Blackberry

Poison Sumac

Woody Nightshade

Eastern Hemlock

Sagebrush

Cecropia Tree

Italian Cypress Tree

Thyme

Khat

Sweet Cherry Tree

New Jersey Tea

Waxmyrtle

White Oak

Black Walnut

Ginkgo Tree

Catalpa Tree

Tree of Heaven

Elderberry

Sweetleaf

European Mistletoe

English Ivy

Balsam Fir Tree   Witch Hazel   Hardhack

Sage

Chinaberry Tree

Bamboo

Weeping Willow Tree

California Laurel Tree

Quaking Aspen Tree

Camphor Tree   Strangler Fig

Castor Oil Shrub

Sassafras Tree

Red Mangrove

Trailing Arbutus

Arizona Cypress

Chaste Tree

American Holly

Japanese Maple

Common Buckthorn

Catawba Rhododendron

Leaves

Leaves

In Myth, Magic, & Medicine

By

ALICE THOMS VITALE

Stewart, Tabori & Chang
New York

Designed by Timothy Shaner

Editorial Director: Linda Sunshine
Editors: Mary Kalamaras, Alexandra Childs,
Melanie Falick, Enid Stubin
Production: Alice Wong

Excerpt from "Indigo" taken from *Indigo and Other
Poems* by Aaron Kramer. Reprinted by permission of
Associated University Presses.

Excerpt from *Flowering Earth* by Donald Culross Peattie
reprinted by permission of Curtis Brown, Ltd.
Copyright © 1942 Donald Culross Peattie.

Library of Congress Cataloging-in-Publication Data

Vitale, Alice Thoms.
Leaves : in myth, magic, and medicine / Alice Thoms
Vitale
p. cm.
Includes bibliographical references.
ISBN 1-55670-554-9
1. Leaves—Folklore. 2. Material medica. Vegetable.
I. Title.
GR780.V57 1997
398'.368—DC20

96-43280
CIP

Published in 1997 by
Stewart, Tabori & Chang,
a division of U.S. Media Holdings, Inc.
115 West 18th Street, New York, New York 10011

Distributed in Canada by
General Publishing Co. Ltd.
30 Lesmill Road, Don Mills
Ontario, Canada M3B 2T6

Distributed in Australia and New Zealand by
Peribo Pty Ltd.
58 Beaumont Road, Mount Kuring-gai
NSW 2080, Australia

Distributed in all other territories by
Grantham Book Services Ltd.
Isaac Newton Way, Alma Park Industrial Estate
Grantham, Linconshire, NG31 9SD England

Publishers Note: Though this book contains numerous methods of healing taken
from ancient herbals, journals, and other
sources, we do not advocate, endorse, or
guarantee the curative effects of any substance listed in this book. We have made
every effort to see that any plant that is poisonous or otherwise potentially dangerous
has been clearly noted as such. The remedies contained within this book are in no
way intended as a substitute for medical
counseling. Please do not attempt self-treatment for minor or serious problems without
first consulting a medical professional or
qualified practitioner.

Printed in Singapore
10 9 8 7 6 5 4 3 2

DEDICATION

This book is dedicated with gratitude and affection to the memory of my parents,
Caroline and Fred Thoms, who, by example, taught me to love every leaf.

TABLE OF CONTENTS

TABLE OF CONTENTS

TABLE OF CONTENTS

TABLE OF CONTENTS

FOREWORD

onald Culross Peattie, known for his sensitive nature writing, expressed precisely and poetically in *Flowering Earth* the fundamental importance of leaves.

"The orator who knows the way to the country's salvation and doesn't know that the breath of life he draws was blown into his nostrils by green leaves, had better spare his breath…The reason for this assertion which I do not make for metaphorical effect, but maintain quite literally, is that the green leaf pigment, chlorophyll, is the one link between the sun and life; it is the conduit of perpetual energy to our own frail organisms. From inert and inorganic elements— water, and carbon dioxide of the air, the same that we breathe out as waste—chlorophyll can synthesize with the energy of sunlight. Every day, every hour of all the ages, as each continent and, equally important, each ocean, rolls into the sunlight, chlorophyll ceaselessly creates. Only when man has done as much, may he call himself the equal of a weed. Plant life sustains

the living world—more precisely, chlorophyll does so. Blood, bone and sinew, all flesh is grass. The wealth and diversity of our material life is accumulated from the primal fact of chlorophyll's activity. The roof of my house, the snapping logs upon the hearth, the desk where I write, are my imports from the plant kingdom. For fundamentally, and away back, coal and oil, gasoline and illuminating gas had green origins too.

We, then, the animals consume those stores in our restless living. Serenely the plants amass them. They turn light's active energy into food, which is potential energy stored for their own benefit. Animal life lives always in the red, obeying the thermodynamic law that energy runs forever downhill. It is the stuff of life that rebels at death. Only chlorophyll fights up against this current. It is the mere cobweb on which we are all suspended over the abyss."

INTRODUCTION

It was with awe
That I beheld
Fresh leaves, green leaves
Bright in the sun.

Basho, 1644–1694

This book is an appreciative salute to the wonder, beauty, and utility of leaves, a visual guide to their identity, with a bow to the woody plants on which they are borne. It is an open window through which can be seen the multifaceted ways, ancient and modern, in which leaves have touched life—human, animal, and, yes, even insect. The wide and interesting diversity of their relationships to life is the focus of this book. It can be described briefly as a world-ranging, historical herbal, a celebration in words and pictures of leaves and their multiple uses—in short, a celebration of the many faces of leaves.

Leaves have inspired our poets and myth-makers, given us nourishment and drink, enriched the flavor of our food, healed us with their medicines, given color to our fabrics, made our gardens, homes, and altars beautiful, and charmed us with their fragrance. Unfortunately, they sometimes also poison and are the source of exhilarating but harmful drugs.

The inclusion of information about leaves used for healing in this book does not constitute an endorsement of possible medicinal value; nor is this book intended as a guide to self-treatment. It is a historical recounting, a backward glance at the ways—valid or not—in which leaves have been used in our long, slow climb toward greater understanding in the science of medicine. Direct quotations from old, even ancient, medical authorities have been included in the text to give the true flavor of the past, an inside look into the former concepts of illness and its healing. Some quotations delight by their very quaintness; others amaze by their long-enduring validity.

These distant voices are those of folk healers, herbalists, and also physicians, all of whom used plants in medical ways. Some of these people may have been charlatans; some were undoubtedly sincere but self-deceived, or limited by their early imperfect knowledge. Others were better informed and more critical, and correctly apprehended certain scientifically founded truths concerning the therapeutic substances contained in plants.

Historically, all plant parts have been used in medicine—leaves, stems, bark, wood, roots, flowers, seeds, and fruit. This volume limits its medicinal scope to the uses of leaves alone, except where other parts are traditionally included with leaves. Some leaves recommended by the healers of the past were worthless or of minimal value, but others were beneficial. Even now, the derivatives of certain leaves—or their synthetic twins—are commonly prescribed. And as another legacy to the world, this old medicine, however flawed or experimental, gave us the beginnings of the related sciences of botany and modern pharmacology.

Today there is a large and growing movement toward further investigation into natural therapeutics from medicinal plants, and to that end, more medical botanists are now inquisitively roaming the earth than ever before. In *Herbs That Heal* (1976), Dr. William Thompson stated that, "In nature is to be found many a secret, the revealing of which has brought to light a healing drug, a soothing balm, or a solace to a distressed mind."

Conversely, as Pierre Joigneaux philosophized more than a century ago, "We have to admit the existence of some absolutely bad plants, created perhaps solely to point out the merits of those that are useful to us, but these absolutely bad plants fortunately are quite rare."

The admonishments about poisons given here in this book are scientifically reliable. Superstitions are mentioned as an entertaining tool for looking into the past. Laughable and ridiculous as they may now seem, they were at one time serious expressions of fears and hopes. Without scientifically developed medicine, superstitions were often the only help to which people could cling.

All of the other relationships to life that are recounted in this book, such as foods and beverages, dyes and drugs, horticulture, crafts, decoration, legends, and poetry, are self-explanatory and need no further elucidation here.

Because some reasonable bounds must be placed on every book, in this one the leaves that perform all these wonders are limited exclusively to those of trees, shrubs, woody vines, a few slightly woody subshrubs, and one vine, kudzu, whose only claim to woodiness is the earth-buried base of the plant. The other exception is bamboo, a grass with woody stems that aspires to be a tree. Of that select group of plants, only those native to America (or if foreign, planted in American parks and gardens) and about which interesting things can be said are included. The only exception is the leaves of nonnative plants not found in America, but whose products and uses are well known to Americans.

Since the appeal of this book is primarily popular, the plants included, forsaking their scientific, taxonomic order, are listed alphabetically under their most prevalent English common names.

In preparing this herbal, the most authentic ancient sources—Biblical, Greek, Roman, Arabic, and Asian—have been searched. Sources less ancient but no less reliable—European, Native American, and American—have also been consulted. The author hopes that this book, an authenticated herbal of the many faces of leaves, with illustrations—genuine portraits created directly from living leaves—will entertain and inform whatever the reader's interest. From botany to horticulture, medicine, history, literature, food, folklore, and handcraft, there is something here for everyone.

THE ILLUSTRATIONS

The printing of natural objects to portray their own image has intrigued people since before recorded time. Even today, remnants of the earliest examples still exist in ancient, painted caves where the distant artists also left impressions of their own pigment-covered hands on the walls. Since that time, many variations on the theme of nature-printing have been developed in ways both simple and direct, as well as complicated and technically advanced.

All of the illustrations in this book are auto prints made from living leaves, portraits which give these representations of nature a unique authenticity. It was with this thought in mind that the book's illustrator—who is also the author—chose an ancient and now little-practiced method of leaf-printing which can be documented historically.

Some interesting early examples still exist; among others, those of a German doctor, Conrad von Butzbach, who in 1425 illuminated the records of his travels by printing the leaves he discovered and, in the same century, Leonardo da Vinci's celebrated *Codex Atlanticus*, which reproduced one small leaf and described the process of coating a leaf with white lead paint and pressing it on blackened paper.

Later, Germans with their characteristic passion for precision, herbalists and botanists, doctors of medicine and pharmacists, produced exact images of leaves, usually those of medicinal plants. Over the years, in that and other countries, some very advanced techniques have been devised, methods involving the processes of photography, lithography, electro- and stero-typing.

In this book, the black-and-white prints of leaves were done by the simplest and most efficient of all methods. Water-based printer's ink was transferred to the surface of fresh leaves with a hand-held rubber roller called a "brayer." The paper for the print was then carefully lowered onto the ink-coated leaves after which the images were obtained by pressing selectively with the thumb (not by rubbing) the paper covering the leaves. Extreme care was the indispensable ingredient. After the shape of the leaves appeared on the paper, the prints were cautiously lifted off and put in a safe place to dry.

All but three of the leaves in this book were hand-gathered by the author in many parts of the world. Three were gifts from others. The coca leaves, all but impossible to obtain legally, were generously sent by Dr. James A. Duke, Taxonomist of the U.S. Agricultural Research Center at Beltsville, Maryland. As he explained, this specimen—dried for several years—no longer contained much, if any, of the forbidden narcotic substances. Though it is difficult to make a print from dried leaves, with special care, it was possible to make just one good picture. After enduring the rigors of printing, these long-dried leaves disintegrated and fell from their twig.

The leaves of the black bamboo were sent by Dr. J. C. Raulston, director of the North Carolina State Arboretum at Raleigh. Though this plant is not native in America, it flourished in North Carolina's mild climate.

And finally, the leaves accompanying the text on tea were a gift from Salvatore Stellato, head of the botanical garden of the University of Naples, Italy.

All of the other specimens of leaves appearing in these illustrations were collected by the author—with permission or without—from Vermont, New York, New Jersey, North Carolina, Florida, Utah, Washington, Oregon, and California. Others came from parks and botanical gardens in Italy— Merano, San Remo, Florence, Rome, Venice and Naples, the islands of Capri, Sardinia, and Sicily. More, too, were found in Spain, Morocco, Austria, and England—wherever the author's wandering feet led her.

THE LEAVES

 green leaf, one of the most fragile and ephemeral of nature's creations, is also one of the most fundamental. Beneath a deceptive simplicity a leaf is a complex source of power for all life.

Typically, a leaf has two parts: the green blade, thin and expanded, and the slender stalk. Also, there is, plainly visible, a network of veins that carry water and mineral salts from the roots to all its parts and also acts as a supportive framework for the leaf's delicate tissue.

Leaves display many shapes and sizes. As Thoreau once correctly observed, "Leaves are of more various forms than the alphabets of all languages put together," and to describe these many variations, a multitude of botanical terms exists. For the purpose of this book, it is essential to mention only the two most basic, simple and compound. A simple leaf is one in which the leaf blade is all in one piece, like the apple leaf; a compound leaf is composed of a number of small leaflets attached to the main leaf stalk, for example, the rose leaf.

Quite different from the broad-bladed leaves are the slender needles—the leaves of the pines, firs, and spruces. Though carrying out the same fundamental functions as other leaves, they are different in form and structure—narrower and frequently harder.

There are also variations of the usual green leaf color, as in the dark red of Japanese maples, some beech trees, and various other trees. In these cases chlorophyll, the green coloring, is present but is overlaid by stronger, darker coloring elements and, therefore, not visible. Golden and other leaf shades also occur.

Though leaves of all kinds are endlessly interesting and wondrous to look at, their primal importance lies in their amazing role in the almost mystic process of photosynthesis. This phenomenal reaction, which takes place within every leaf, is the most creative and life-supportive on earth. There is, in fact, no living thing that could exist in the world as we know it without green leaves to capture the sun's energy. Every day leaves are endlessly working, seizing, storing, converting, and utilizing the sun's energy.

Within the tissue of every leaf there are cells composed of different pigments of which chlorophyll is the most important. It is the abundant presence of chlorophyll that gives leaves their characteristic green color that, indeed, colors our world green.

It is this verdant substance, contained in corpuscles called chloroplasts, that seizes the energy of light from the sun and combines it with carbon dioxide from the atmosphere and with water containing mineral salts sent up by the roots. This complex process, starting a long chain reaction, produces the organic substances sugar and starch, which become life-energy for the plant, enabling it to grow and to create still more leaves, and also flowers, fruit, wood, and roots. The benefits of this creative action are then bestowed on animals, including humans, who consume or otherwise utilize these plant products.

The extraordinary work of leaves does not end with the creation of sugar and starch; it is also the source of the life-sustaining oxygen in the air we breathe. There is in the carbon dioxide and the water utilized by the leaves during photosynthesis more oxygen than is actually needed. The excess oxygen is liberated into the air by the leaves, and this wealth of oxygen is the very breath of life to all on earth.

There is a small, intriguing, and most remarkable fact to ponder about chlorophyll—namely, the close resemblance between hemin, the red pigment in the blood of animals, and chlorophyll, the green coloring in leaves. The chemical structures of these two vital substances are fundamentally the same, except where chlorophyll contains magnesium, the hemin of blood contains iron. This similarity points to the close relationship between plants and animals, the basic oneness of all life.

The life-nurturing work of leaves continues even after they die and fall to the ground. With the aid of bacteria, fungi, insects, and moisture, leaves decompose into nutrient humus, enriching the soil for future generations of plants that, in turn, will do the same, thus endlessly renewing the earth.

AUTHOR'S NOTE

There surely will be some who, when reading this book about leaves, will wonder why so much has been quoted from the words and ideas of the ancients, among them the Greeks Dioscorides, Hippocrates, and Theophrastus, and the Roman Pliny. Others, too, are included, but are of lesser antiquity—the Englishmen Gerard, Parkinson, and Culpeper, the learned Swedes, Linnaeus and Kalm, and the Italian Mattioli.

In depicting the myriad ways leaves have touched life, these authorities must be credited. These people all lived in times when leaves, simple leaves, had a direct and telling effect on lives, on medicine, on the ideas—today we would call them superstitions—and customs people lived by. Today the ideas and legends that once surrounded leaves have been overshadowed—sometimes eliminated by—science and its advanced technology.

Often we, the inheritors of the old knowledge, appreciate leaves—if we think of them at all—only for their beauty in parks and gardens, their cooling shade, their splendid autumn color, their soothing sounds as they stir in the breeze, and, for certain leaves, their fragrance. And though we never consciously appreciate that greatest of all treasures that leaves bestow, we take into our lungs with every breath the oxygen that they in their mysterious botanical function release into the air.

But there is more—much more—the details of which time has hidden in leaves. Along with much other information, this book uncovers these olden secrets.

Every leaf a miracle.
—Walt Whitman

Now as I was young and easy under the apple boughs
About the lilting house and happy as the grass was green.

—Dylan Thomas, Fern Hill

Apple Tree

APPLE TREE

Apple Tree   *Malus pumila*   (Rose Family)

Behold the remarkable, beauteous, nourishing apple tree. Soft with spring bloom, it charms and delights; heavy with autumn fruit, it promises fine food and drink.

Originally from west Asia and Europe, the ancient common apple tree is the ancestor of the most modern varieties of edible apples. Now the most important, best-known fruit tree of cool temperate zones, it is extensively planted by commercial growers and home gardeners.

Apple seeds contain cyanide and eating a cupful of them has caused cyanide poisoning.

The tree's sweet fruit—green, yellow, russet, and red—is its finest gift. The seldom available but handsome wood is prized for furniture. And formerly the leaves were also considered useful, though limited.

They were mentioned medicinally by the ancient Greek physician Dioscorides who said, "The leaves and blossoms and sprigs of all sorts of apple trees are binding." Fifteen centuries later, the English herbalist John Gerard, repeated, "The leaves of the tree do coole and binde, and also be good for inflammations in the beginning." This meager medical information and a mention of the leaves as flavoring for vodka seem to be their sole distinction.

*

In America, however, the one-time proliferation of these trees—and therefore, of their leaves—is the subject of the famous and enduring legend of Johnny Appleseed.

*

Born in 1774, John Chapman, later called "Johnny Appleseed," was a dedicated, eccentric nurseryman with a compelling mission. Raising, planting, and distributing apple trees was his life's passion. Many believe that he only "gave" away his trees, but actually, he charged a "flip penny bit" (six cents) for

a sapling or sold them for uncollected promissory notes; he also accepted used clothing as payment. When poor farmers couldn't pay, he then gave away his trees.

*

The seeds for these trees he collected from cider presses in Pennsylvania, transporting them westward in bags on his back, on horseback, or sometimes in canoes. While roaming the Ohio River valley, he planted more than thirty-five orchards in Ohio, Indiana, and Illinois.

*

His generosity, uncouth appearance, and odd clothes all have contributed to this apple-tree legend. In addition, he was uncommonly kind, cheerful, friendly with the Native Americans, knowledgeable about herbal medicine—and a religious Swedenborgian.

*

In 1845, after years of exhausting walk-

Wassailing—the practice of wishing good health and a bountiful harvest for fruit trees—is a centuries-old English custom still practiced in some cider orchards today. The largest apple tree in the orchard is selected and then celebrated by throwing cider on its trunk.

ing—ill clad, ill
shod, poorly protect-
ed from the weather,
often sleeping under
the stars—Johnny
Appleseed died in
Indiana, presumably of
exposure. The words on his
gravestone read—"He lived
for others."

As the apple tree among the trees of the
wood, so is my beloved among the sons.

—The Song of Solomon 2:3

I believe in the forest, and in the meadow, and in
the night in which the corn grows. We require an
infusion of hemlock-spruce or arbor-vitae in our tea.

—Henry David Thoreau, Walking

Arbor Vitae

ARBOR VITAE

Arbor Vitae   *Thuja occidentalis*   (Cypress Family)

The aromatic arbor vitae, Latin for "Tree of Life," is well named. Native to the cool northern forests of America, this tree has truly been a source of life for all. Many animals, including deer, moose, and hare, find food and shelter in its groves; the Native Americans healed with its medicine; the pioneers shingled their homes with its wood. And husky north-woods loggers concocted a strength-giving drink from its leaves, singing its praises in a lusty song:

> A quart of Arbor Vitae
> To make him strong and mighty.

🌿

Even before the arrival of Europeans to America, the Native Americans had discovered many life-preserving uses for arbor vitae. Leaves boiled in bear grease made a salve for skin disorders, including warts and fungoid ailments. It was also effective as a counterirritant for the relief of rheumatism. Leaves in tea were a remedy for headaches, coughs, fevers, gout, and catarrh, and also served as a blood purifier. Even the smoke of burning leaves was used for healing, for inducing perspiration, for reviving the unconscious, and especially for the exorcising of evil spirits. Perhaps arbor vitae's most convincing success was its cure for scurvy, once a common wintertime deficiency disease.

🌿

It is said that while the French

~ 35 ~

navigator Jacques Cartier was exploring the St. Lawrence River, he met a Native American named Domagaia who taught him how to make a decoction of arbor vitae to cure his men of scurvy. Domagaia advised him "to take the barke and leaves of the sayd tree, and boile them together, then to drink of the sayd decoction every other day, and to put the dregs of it upon his legs that

is sick." Vitamin C, as such, had not yet been discovered, but the therapeutic power of arbor vitae for remedying its lack was already known.

❧

When word of this "wonder tree" reached England, arbor vitae became one of the first trees from America north of Mexico to be introduced into Europe.

❧

From 1942 to 1952 the *U.S. Pharmacopoeia* recognized arbor vitae's powerful oil as a diuretic, a stimulant for heart and uterine muscles, a counterirritant, and an antiseptic.

❧

Today, the oil, with its intense, penetrating odor, is an active ingredient in insect repellents. Its clean, spicy fragrance scents soaps and other toilet preparations, room deodorizers, and even costly perfumes.

An old Chinese cure for baldness calls for steeping fresh arbor vitae leaves for one week in a 60% alcohol solution. To promote hair growth, this solution would be rubbed into bald spots three times per day.

TRAILING ARBUTUS

Trailing Arbutus   *Epigaea repens*   (Heath Family)

Guided by its sweet perfume,
I found, within a narrow dell,
The trailing spring flower tinted like a shell
Amid dry leaves and mosses at my feet.

In these few words, the American poet John Greenleaf Whittier captured the very essence of the trailing arbutus—the fragrance, the delicate color of the blossoms, and its concealed manner of growing. Those who know this plant delight in discovering it in the dormant woods of the earliest spring, hidden by the preceding year's dead leaves but secretly alive and fragrantly blooming, sometimes even beneath the lingering remains of late snow.

People frequently seek it not only for the beauty of the modest blossoms but also for its pure fragrance unmatched by any other. Though supposedly it is a plant protected by law, greedy searchers still destructively tear it from the earth, and, as a result, it verges on extinction in some areas.

In the past, evergreen leaves of trailing arbutus were a trusted remedy for urinary problems. The Shakers, knowledgeable specialists in the medical botany of

Trailing Arbutus

early America, recom-
mended as a remedy an
infusion of one ounce of
leaves in
one quart
of boiling
water. For
inflammation of
the bladder, related
infections, and even blood
in the urine, the leaves, either
fresh with alcohol or dried in
infusions, were prescribed.

An alternate name, gravel
plant, gives a clue to another of the herbal benefits of
trailing arbutus: for destroying,
or possibly even preventing, painful
calculi—stones or gravel in the bladder
or kidneys. Even today the medicinal
qualities of trailing arbutus and other
plants in the Heath family are considered genuinely valid.

QUAKING ASPEN

Quaking Aspen   *Populus tremula*   (Willow Family)

In the upland forests of the American West, the quaking aspen is the glory of autumn. Glowing in all shades of gold—from pale to gilt to warm bronze—the leaves flutter incessantly in the wind because of their uniquely flattened stems. Against the background of somber evergreens, spruces, and pines, the quivering, golden flames of the aspen light the surrounding hills even when the day is dark. Although the aspen is the most widespread tree in America, found from the Atlantic to the Pacific, it is most abundant in the West, where it grows the tallest and where the autumn splendor of its leaves is most brilliant.

Not only has the colorful beauty of the aspen attracted attention, but the perpetual quaking of its leaves has raised questions and prompted speculative answers. In countries where the closely related European aspen grows—and also trembles—fanciful explanations have attempted to account for this nervous fluttering. In France, according to one religious belief, aspen leaves shook with fear because Christ's cross on Calvary was made from this wood. In Germany, a legend told that the aspen tree was cursed by Jesus because during the flight into Egypt, it alone refused to acknowledge him, and when he spoke,

Aspen trees are one of the first tree species to repopulate an area that has been cleared by fire or cutting; groves can return to their original numbers in as little as fifty years.

the tree began to tremble. Another imaginative explanation maintained that aspen leaves are made from women's tongues which, according to some, are always wagging.

✼

This tree and its ever-moving leaves were once a magical, medical cure. A now obsolete system of healing called the Doctrine of Signatures claimed that illnesses could be cured with plants having the same form as the ailing part of the body, or exhibiting the same symptoms as the disease. Thus the aspen, with its shak-

ing leaves, was the plant especially designated to heal ague, or shaking palsy. Following this belief, early folk healers in England advised a patient with palsy to pin a lock of his or her hair to an aspen tree while repeating:

> Aspen tree, aspen tree
> I prithee shiver and shake
> Instead of me.

The ill person was then to walk home in silence, or the spell would be broken and the cure would fail.

✼

The bark of the aspen, like the willow, contains analgesic and anti-inflammatory properties. Native American women would drink a tea made from it to ease menstrual cramps. This tea also aided in alleviating diarrhea and urinary disorders.

✼

A poultice made from the root of the aspen was often used for cuts and bruises.

Quaking Aspen

And the wind full of wantonness
Woos like a lover
The young Aspen trees
Till they tremble all over.

—Thomas Moore
Lalla Rookh, Light of
the Harem

BALSAM FIR

Balsam Fir   *Abies balsamea*   (Pine Family)

The balsam fir, disliked by loggers for lumber, is prized by Americans as a Christmas tree because of its symmetrical spire, its long-lasting greenery, and its spicy, resinous odor. All parts of the tree are fragrant; the sap, the bark and wood, and the blunt-tipped needles all release their inimitable aroma into the surrounding air. This heady perfume is so closely associated with the Christmas season that one breath of this woodland bouquet recreates in the mind the lights, carols, gifts, and family memories of holidays past.

In northern Europe the fir tree has been an important part of Christmas festivities since the Middle Ages, when it was considered a Christian symbol of everlasting life.

St. Boniface, an eighth-century missionary to the Druidic Germans, reputedly wrote these words recommending the fir tree as a symbol of Christianity, and of its holiest festival. "This little tree, a young child of the forest, shall be your holy tree tonight. It is the wood of peace, for your houses are built of the fir. It is the sign of an endless life, for its leaves are ever green. See how it points upward to heaven. Let this be called the tree of the Christ-child. Gather around it, not in the wild-wood, but in your own homes."

While our holiday use of the fir came to us from Europe, the Native Americans, quite uninfluenced by European traditions, also valued it; for them the balsam fir was a green medicine.

Dictionaries define balsam as an aromatic substance that heals and soothes, which is precisely how the Native Americans put the needles of this tree to use. The Ojibwas used an essence created from these sweet-scented leaves as a reviver for those who had lost consciousness. Other Native Americans used fresh balsam needles as a healing balm for colds or coughs by placing them in a sweat bath on hot coals so their fumes could be inhaled. Today, this is called a Turkish bath.

Currently, the medicinal virtues of balsam needles are forgotten; instead, in Adirondack Mountain souvenir shops, tourists buy small balsam-filled pillows inscribed with this simple country rhyme:

> *I miss you in the summer,*
> *I miss you in the fall, some,*
> *But specially at Christmas time,*
> *I pine, fir, yew and balsam.*

While some in the past believed the fir a soothing medicinal, others relied on the comforting superstitions that surrounded it. A green branch laid across a bed prevented nightmares; hung over a barn door, it kept evil spirits from stealing the grain.

Balsam Fir

Bamboo

BLACK BAMBOO

Black Bamboo   *Phyllostachys nigra*   (Grass Family)

amboo: poets praise it, artists paint it, still others call it one of the world's most useful plants. From dwarfs of a few inches to towering giants, bamboo, botanically, is not a tree; it's an arborescent, or tree-like, grass. Because it is woody-stemmed with uses usually reserved for trees, it is included here with trees and shrubs.

Growing in clumps like most grasses, the tallest bamboos inhabit tropical Asian forests. Other bamboos introduced into the United States flourish as far north as Virginia, while a few have adapted to even colder climates. There are also small, native American bamboos.

This plant of strange habits and countless uses blooms only after many years, flowering at infrequent intervals, sometimes only once every sixty years. In Asia the ripe seeds are eaten as grain, the young shoots as vegetables, and though certain species of bamboo are poisonous when raw, they become safe after cooking. Tabasheer, or bamboo sugar—a substance found in the joints of bamboo—has long been recognized in Asian medicine as a relief for coughs. The woody stems are fashioned into furniture, fences, flutes, and more, while fibers and pulp are made into paper.

Bamboo is important to humans, but for the rare giant panda, bamboo is vital for its survival. Though scientifically classed a carnivore, the panda actually lives almost exclusively on a vegetable diet, of which ninety-five percent is bamboo foliage.

⁂

The way the panda holds its daily ration of bamboo is unique. While it has the mammal's typical five digits, none can be rotated for grasping like the human thumb. Instead the panda grasps the foliage with a small spur on its wrist bone, then pushes it into the side of its mouth, crushing the leaves and stems with its

Many people do not know that Thomas A. Edison experimented successfully with using bamboo as a filament for the incandescent light bulb. In fact, bulbs with bamboo filaments were manufactured as late as 1910.

powerful molars.

⁂

Inexplicably, the panda's favorite species of bamboo dies off about every one hundred years, and though the plants eventually replenish themselves, before they do, many pandas perish from starvation. Formerly, when this die-off occurred, pandas simply moved into another bamboo-rich valley, but now with China's vast population, they are trapped in a sea of humanity where they can find neither the bamboo nor the isolation necessary for their lives. Because the devastating bamboo famine is expected to recur soon, the World Wildlife Fund has declared the few remaining pandas (about one thousand) as one of the world's ten most endangered species.

⁂

SWEET BAY

Bay/Sweet Bay/True Laurel   *Laurus nobilis*   (Laurel Family)

For two thousand years, the fragrant leaves of the sweet bay tree, or true laurel, have charmed, sustained, healed, honored, and protected humans in thousands of ways. In praise of these wondrous leaves, English herbalist John Parkinson wrote, "The bay leaves are of as necessary use as any in the garden or orchard; they serve both for ornament and use, for honest civil uses and for physic [medicine], yea both for the sick and the sound, for the living and the dead...from the cradle to the grave, we still have use of it, we still have need of it." It has never been said better.

❦

An old myth tells of the origin of this tree, which was sacred to the ancient Greeks. The god Apollo, upon seeing the nymph Daphne, fell immediately in love and pursued her. However, because she had once been struck by Cupid's leaden arrow—according to this tale—she could love neither god nor mortal. As Apollo approached, she called upon her river-god father, Peneus, to save her. Magically, he then changed her into a laurel tree. Though rejected and disappointed in love, Apollo took this tree as his symbol, decreeing that it should be hallowed and remain everlastingly green. He further proclaimed that all who excel in courage, civil service, or the creation of beauty should be crowned with laurel leaves so that their memories might remain ever green.

While the lives of the gods were intertwined with these leaves, mortals, too, have been touched by their magic. Superstitions have credited laurel (bay) with protective powers—against witches, the devil, and lightning. Because laurel was said to repel death, a green branch was hung on the door of the seriously ill. English midwives rubbed laurel leaves on the feet of babies born feet first, to protect these "footlings" who were believed susceptible to laming accidents.

BAY RUM COLOGNE

2-1/2 ounces bay leaves, crushed
1-1/2 tsp. ground cardamom
1/2 tsp. ground cinnamon
1/2 tsp. ground cloves
1 pint Jamaican rum

Add bay leaves and spices to the rum and shake well. Strain and bottle. This cologne will stay true for months if kept at room temperature.

Roman emperor Tiberius had a phobic fear of lightning and always wore a wreath of bay during thunderstorms since it was believed that lightning never struck the bay tree.

Considered a potent medicine, laurel leaves in teas, baths, poultices, and ointments healed the "stingings of waspes and bees," helped to "weish out freckles," were effective for removing pimples, for banishing rheumatism— even for warding off the plague. The list of its reputed powers has over time included curing pain, deafness, sprains, headache, colic, coughs, obstructed livers, even epilepsy.

Laurel (bay) leaves are no longer holy, but domestic uses for them abound. Their savory flavor enhances food and their powerful odor banishes moths and fleas and lends fragrance to soaps and perfumes. As Parkinson once said, "We still have need of them."

Sweet Bay

PAPER BIRCH

Paper Birch   *Betula papyrifera*   (Birch Family)

The paper birch, slender and elegant, traces a vivid white line against the dark evergreens of northern forests. Its bark, blinding-bright in the sunlight, is so intensely white that it is visible even in the dark of night.

❋

The tough outer wrapping of this tree, which is golden on the inside, is the bark from which America's northeastern Indians fashioned their strong, light bark canoes—as lines from Longfellow's "Song of Hiawatha" tell.

> Give me of your bark, O Birch tree,
> Of your yellow bark, O birch tree,
> I, a light canoe will build me
> That shall float upon the water
> Like a yellow water lily.

❋

Native Americans, early American colonists, and European herbalists all agreed that birch leaves were therapeutic and all prescribed them for the same disorders. They administered strong infusions or the expressed juice of young leaves as diuretics, for breaking stones of kidney and bladder, and to relieve gout, rheumatism, and dropsy. Because birch leaves are composed of natural astringents, contracting tissues, they arrest the discharge of fluids, and were, therefore, considered an effective treatment for many skin problems, including eruptions, scurvy, and burns; dry leaves and

In Scandinavian lore, the god Thor considered the birch tree sacred and those who hung its branches inside their homes were protected from the evil eye, lightning, and infertility.

fine twigs were ground to a soothing powder and were dusted on chafed skin. Decoctions of leaves healed raw, sore throats, calmed irritations of the stomach and intestines, and reduced fevers.

❧

Birch leaves are still believed to be therapeutic today. Weleda, a reputable Swiss pharmaceutical firm, combines young birch leaves with lemon juice to create an elixir to cleanse the blood of impurities deposited by a sluggish metabolism.

❧

The leaves and twigs of the fragrant black birch boast a spicy aroma and are used to make a scented oil that is sometimes added to medicines to disguise their disagreeable taste.

❧

Recently, these useful and luminous birch trees have embarked on a prestigious new career. Because of their singular beauty, they have been designated National Memorial Trees for Mothers and as such were planted on the Capitol grounds in Washington, D.C. One located in Arlington National Cemetery in Virginia has been named the National Mothers' Tree.

Paper Birch

Weeping Birch

WEEPING WHITE BIRCH

Weeping White Birch   *Betula alba var. dalecarlica*   (Birch Family)

his European birch, a slim ornamental tree with elegant leaves, pendant branches, and pale silvery bark, is a living jewel in American gardens. Coming originally from Sweden and cool parts of Asia, it is essentially a northern tree.

❦

The delicately formed leaves, which are irregularly cut and end in curved tips, are the unique beauty of this tree. Enchanting as they are at any season because of their graceful shape, these leaves become even more lovely in

> *In the Victorian language of flowers, the birch symbolizes grace and meekness.*

autumn when, hanging from their pendulous branches, they form a fringed curtain of gold.

❦

Though the value of weeping birch leaves has remained primarily aesthetic, who among us would deny that, while intangible, this is a very real contribution to life. Gerard, a sixteenth-century English herbalist and author of the still famous *Herbal*, had his own way of expressing this wisdom. In speaking of certain plants, beautiful but of little genuine practical value, he sagely said, "These plants are not used in meat [food] or medicine, but are esteemed for their beauty to decke up gardens, the bosomes of the beautiful, garlands and crowns for pleasure."

Expressing this same thought, Robert Frost wrote three hundred years later in *The Young Birch*: "It was a thing of beauty, and was sent to live its life out as an ornament."

For a refreshing skin wash, add a palmful of fresh birch leaves to a cup of boiling water. Remove from heat and steep for two to three minutes. To combat acne, make the solution stronger by boiling the leaves for five to eight minutes.

"The birch path is one of the prettiest places in the world." It was. Other people besides Anne thought so when they stumbled on it. It was a little narrow, twisting path, winding down over a long hill straight through Mr. Bell's woods, where light came down sifted through so many emerald screens that it was as flawless as the heart of a diamond. It was fringed in all its length with slim young birches, white-stemmed, and starflowers and wild lilies-of-the-valley and scarlet tufts of pigeon berries grew thickly along it; and always there was a delightful spiciness in the air and music of bird calls and the murmur and laugh of wood winds in the trees overhead.

—L. M. Montgomery,
Anne of Green Gables

BITTERSWEET

Bittersweet   *Celastrus scandens*   (Staff-Tree Family)

The word "bittersweet" recalls to mind crisp autumn weather and day-trips into the country in search of branches, seed-pods, berries, and dried grasses for long-lasting bouquets. The woods, fields, hedgerows, and stone walls yielded up treasures for winter-keeping, and one of the most coveted finds was bright-berried bit-tersweet. In those carefree days before our present conservational awareness, picking bittersweet was common, but it is now illegal and the tree can only be admired where it grows in its natural habitat, festooning shrubs or scrambling over old fences and stone walls. However, in spite of these nature-pro-tecting regulations, the hanging clusters

of bright autumn berries are still a sore temptation, visually luring people to plunder the vines.

❦

Of bittersweet, Nicholas Culpeper wrote in his herbal, "It is excellently good to remove witchcraft both in men and beasts, as also all sudden diseases whatsoever... Country people commonly take the berries of it, and having bruised them, apply them to felons, and thereby soon rid their fingers of such trouble-some guests."

❦

For deer, early summer bittersweet leaves are an irresistible enticement. Aldo Leopold, one of America's great naturalists, recounted in his *Sand*

County Almanac a strange, almost mystical occurrence. "I like the bittersweet," he wrote, "because my father did, and because deer, on the first of July each year, begin suddenly to eat the new leaves, and I have learned to predict this event to my guests. I cannot dislike a plant that enables me, a mere professor, to blossom forth annually as a successful seer and prophet."

This rambling, woody vine, sometimes also called false bittersweet and waxwork, grows wild in the eastern and central United States and bears orange autumn fruit that, when ripe, bursts open to reveal a brilliant scarlet berry. Also available from nurseries, this berried, native vine is in fact, so decorative that gardeners plant it as an ornamental.

Note: The solid black leaf in this illustration was printed from the right, or top side of the leaf; the others, with veins clearly visible, were printed from the underside.

Bittersweet

BLACKBERRY

Blackberry Species   *Rubus spp.*   (Rose Family)

This slender creeping vine has wide-open white flowers proclaiming a kinship to roses. Other blackberries are thorny, tangled shrubs belonging to an endlessly varied plant group. Originally totaling about twenty species, by crossing and recrossing, the number of varieties has now increased to thousands. While their classification perplexes botanists, the fruit itself is commonly recognized by most Americans. These black, seedy berries are gathered for jams, pies, and that distilled delight, blackberry brandy.

These spiny plants, which now flourish in many parts of the world, were also known in ancient Greece. The Greek physician Dioscorides prescribed blackberry leaves for strengthening the gums, for healing hemorrhoids and ulcers, and for heart and stomach trouble.

Later, in England, another healer named John Gerard quaintly claimed in his *Herbal*, "They heale the eyes that hang out, and hard knots in the fundament [buttocks]." Continuing, he said, "The leaves boiled in water with honey, alum, and a little white wine added, fastneth the teeth"—if true, an amazing bit of dental advice.

English folk medicine rightly recommended these tannin-rich leaves as a remedy for burns, claiming they were most effective when accompanied by this spoken charm:

There came three angels out of the east,
One brought fire, two brought frost.
Out fire and in frost
In the name of the Father, Son
and Holy Ghost.

The English settlers in the New World prescribed astringent blackberry leaves in decoctions for diarrhea, dysentery, and as a healing gargle for sore throats. Later, when these colonists revolted against England, and imported tea became costly and unpatriotic, they drank a substitute tea of blackberry leaves, which was both wholesome and palatable. Early Americans with a taste for stronger drink made a wine of young leaves and new tips. Boiled with sugar and set aside for a year before drinking, it was a pleasant if not truly exciting beverage.

While appreciation of the white roselike flowers and sweet but seedy black fruit has in no way changed or diminished over time, the leaves of the blackberry plant no longer enjoy their former prestige. They are used, however, as a natural dye for wool by some crafts-people, and wild food enthusiasts eat the young leaves in salads.

BLACKBERRY CORDIAL

2 quarts ripe blackberries
1 pint of desired brandy

Using a food processor, mash the berries, taking care not to overprocess. Place in a container large enough to hold berries and brandy. Add the brandy, seal container, and let stand, undisturbed, in a cool, dry place for 3 to 4 weeks. Strain the liquid and bottle.

The leaves being chewed do strengthen ye gums...and heal ye running ulcers and haemorrhoids...it is available for ye stomachical and ye cardiacal being beaten small and so laid on.

—Greek Herbal of Dioscorides

And the running blackberry,
Would adorn the parlors of heaven.

—Walt Whitman
Song of Myself

Blackberry

BO TREE

Bo Tree   *Ficus religiosa*   (Mulberry Family)

The Indian bo tree, with its long-tailed leaves that continually flutter on long, slim stems, has a celebrated history rich in religious legend. Because of its ancient links to faith, Linnaeus, the famed Swedish botanist and plant-namer, called this tree—a member of the vast Fig genus—*Ficus religiosa*, or the religious fig.

❊

Hindus often depict Vishnu — one god in their triad of deities—seated on the revered leaves of the bo tree. However, the tree's achievement of greatest renown came when Prince Siddartha Gautama—who later became the Buddha—sat beneath its branches, meditating on the meaning of existence. It was there, sheltered by its constantly trembling leaves, that he achieved nirvana, or divine enlightenment, an experience that inspired him in 528 B.C. to found a new religion. Today, Buddhism is one of the five great religions of the world. For its role in the Buddha's enlightenment, the bo tree is deeply venerated, and Bodhgaya, India, where it grew, is now a sacred place of pilgrimage for Buddhists.

❊

The large tree standing there today is believed by the faithful to be a direct descendant, having been successively repropagated by trees whose seeds are traced back to the original bo tree. The tree's alternate name, bodhi, refers to that historic event and means tree of enlightenment or awakening; buddha signifies Enlightenment or Awakened One.

❖

There are mundane and immediately practical uses as well in India for these leaves—as nourishing green fodder for elephants, and as an alternate food for silkworms.

❖

Here in America, in warm parts of Florida and California, the leaves of the bo tree, which was introduced into this country in the twentieth century, flutter in every breeze as they once did when they cast their quivering shade on the sacred Buddha.

In India, the sacred bo tree is revered as the source for soma, the drink of immortality. Each time the new moon falls on a Monday (Somavara) the tree is honored by the rite of somavati, a ritual practiced by the women of Maharashtra.

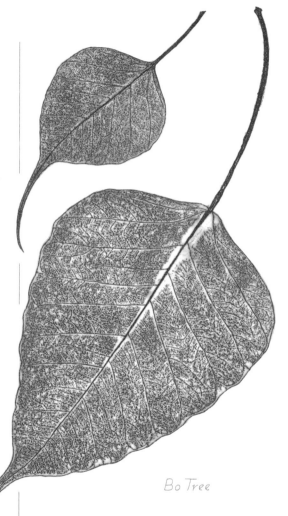

Bo Tree

COMMON BOX

Common Box   *Buxus sempervirens*   (Box Family)

ow can you describe the strange odor of box? This old scent has often been tentatively described as "catlike," or, "of an evil and loathesome smell." Oliver Wendell Holmes, an American philosopher, described it mystically. "Box," he said, "has the flavor of eternity." This odor so difficult to describe is, indeed, unusual—and unforgettable.

But more than for its indescribable fragrance, box—an evergreen shrub with myriad small leaves crowded on thin twigs—is valued for handsome hedges. The close-leafed box is also ideal for topiary work, beloved by Victorian gardeners, for carving into birds, animals, gargoyles, and other strange green creatures.

A fantastic old legend told that a decoction of these box leaves together with the dust of its wood boiled in lye would promote a thick growth of hair, also giving the hair an auburn color. This quaint but unlikely story described a young Silesian girl who had lost all her hair because of a malignant dysentery.

Upon learning that this box-leaf concoction would restore it, she washed her head with the magic mixture, which, as promised, actually did cause her hair  to return—luxuriantly. However, she had carelessly failed to protect her face, neck, and shoulders from this hair-promoting remedy, and as a result, she was soon so covered with red hair that she resembled a hirsute ape.

❦

Box leaves are scientifically known as the source of dangerous compounds, notably the deadly alkaloid buxine. Though most domestic animals avoid eating this green forage, pigs—either brainless or unprotected by instinct—have been known to eat hedge clippings with fatal results.

❦

And, as with some other poisonous plants, box has been employed medicinally. A veterinary remedy was formerly made from these leaves for treating horses infested with bots—the parasitical larvae of the botfly that affect the digestive organs. Powdered box leaves, even recently, were given to horses to improve their coats. More importantly, modern tests have shown that the alkaloids in box leaves actually contain tumor-inhibiting properties.

❦

In old England, after Christmas holly and other holiday greens were removed from churches and homes, branches of box were put up until Easter. Robert Herrick, an English poet, recalling this custom, wrote:

Down with Rosemary and Bayes,
Down with Mistletoe.
Instead of Holly, now upraise
The greener Box for show.

❦

Common Box

The Box tree groweth greene winter and summer.
—John Gerard, The Herbal

BUCKTHORN

Common Buckthorn   *Rhamnus catharticus*   (Buckthorn Family)

Has someone cast a spell on you? To compensate, hang leafy buckthorn branches in your home. This was the advice of Pierandrea Mattioli, a sixteenth-century Italian physician and herbalist who cautiously wrote, "They say the branches [of buckthorn], when put at the doors and windows of houses, drive away all sorceries and enchantments."

❧

These powerful shrubs grow wild in Greece. Dioscorides, the first-century physician, claimed these leaves "are an excellent remedy for eczema and erysipelas," inflammatory skin diseases. Today in Greece, there is a small town whose name, Ramnous, celebrates these protective and therapeutic leaves, which are borne on the shrubs that blanket the encircling hills.

❧

The common buckthorn, though now growing wild in the eastern United States, came originally, in some way now lost to memory, from Asia and southern Europe. Here, its leaves, bark, and black berries were sometimes given as a strong, even harsh, purgative, but its use was limited because in addition to the violent reaction it can bring on, it also has an unpleasantly bitter taste. There have also been occasional reports of poisoning resulting from the use of this buckthorn as a cathartic, or severe laxative. American buckthorn *(Rhamnus purshiana)*, native to the northwestern coastal region, is the source of *Cascara sagrada*, an effective but milder and less irritating laxative.

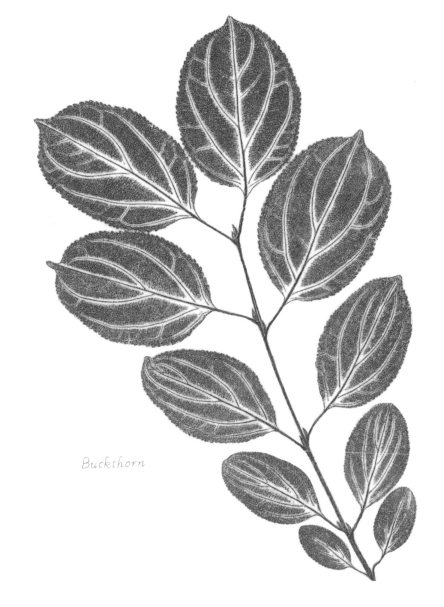

Buckthorn

CAJEPUT

Cajeput/Melaleuca   *Melaleuca quinquenervia*   (Myrtle Family)

An explosive invasion of the Everglades by the beautiful cajeput tree is threatening Florida's wildlife. In the mistaken hope of transforming what were in the 1940s deemed "useless" wetlands into timber-producing areas, the seeds of this Australian tree were sown by air. This aerial seeding, along with the acceleration of canal digging and subsequent drainage of the swamps, triggered a destructive attack that has ruthlessly crowded out the native vegetation so essential for supporting animal life. Now, fifty years later, the results of that sowing are appallingly apparent.

So far biologists at the Everglades National Park have found no way to curb the proliferation of these trees. To quote one of these scientists, "Melaleuca [cajeput] is one of the most serious long-term threats to the park. Water is a big problem, but this could be worse."

This controversial, imported tree is conspicuously attractive, its dark green leaves a pleasing contrast to its pale, papery bark. Home gardeners believe that the strong odor emitted by the leaves keeps insects away; some even claim that the protective effect from the leaves also extends to other nearby plants. For these reasons, it has been extensively planted as a lawn and street tree in Florida.

Cajeput

But disturbing new information has recently surfaced. Because irritating allergens have been identified in the pollen of the flowers of the cajeput tree, some Florida communities are now banning it from public parks and gardens.

❦

However, in places where this tree is native, such as Australia, the Molucca Islands, and other nearby areas, people hold it in high esteem. The oil commercially produced from fresh leaves and twigs is considered an almost universal remedy for an endless chronicle of aches and pains. Applied externally, it calms rheumatism, neuralgia, sprains, bruises, toothaches, and earaches. Internally, in doses of one to ten drops on sugar, it is reportedly effective for colic, spasms, flatulence, hiccups, and as a stimulating expectorant. A few drops on a soft cloth when allowed to evaporate near the eyes relieves their irritation. As a parasiticide, this oil, diluted with olive oil, quells itching, scabies, psoriasis, and other skin complaints. Even violent headaches subside when it is inhaled or rubbed on the temples.

❦

This sovereign remedy, however, comes with a warning. An overdose of this volatile substance, taken internally, can cause gastrointestinal irritation and, even worse, dangerous inflammation of the kidneys. Like many other valuable plants, this tree and its leaves and their medicine are both benevolent and malevolent.

❦

CALIFORNIA LAUREL

California Laurel   *Umbellularia californica*   (Laurel Family)

alifornians proudly call this handsome tree the California laurel, while Oregonians have dubbed it the Oregon myrtle. And these are only the most common of its dozen or so names, most of them making reference to its strong, sweet, but also spicy, almost camphor-like, perfume. Among them are spice tree, pepperwood, and the most fanciful, balm of heaven.

All parts of this tree are odorous—the twigs, bark, flowers, olive-like fruit, golden, mottled wood, and, most of all, leaves.

Pick a leaf, crush it lightly, but smell it very, very gently. Inhaled too suddenly

Beware that your Northern laurels do not change to Southern willows.

—*Charles Lee to General Horatio Gates after the surrender of Burgoyne at Saratoga, October 17, 1777.*

and too deeply, it can cause the same sharp, intense pain as accidentally breathing in a noseful of water while swimming, a sensation which inspired one man to say, "This tree is a pain in the nose."

Green medicine hides in strong-smelling laurel leaves. The Native Americans of the West taught the pioneers to bind California laurel leaves around their heads to relieve headaches, and to wrap them around

their bodies for chronic stomach trouble. These early settlers also treated other internal ailments with hot teas made from fresh leaves. They eased their rheumatism with steamy baths thick with pungent leaves, and cleared congested sinuses by cautiously sniffing the potent vapors. A distillation of leaves and wood, a once-recommended remedy for treating catarrh, colic, diarrhea, even meningitis, was later deemed ineffective.

❧

Native Americans in California, aware that intense odors repel insects, rubbed the leaves of this native tree on their skin, or scattered them in their dwellings to ban fleas, mosquitoes, and other biting bugs—practical informa-

In the language of flowers, the California laurel has come to symbolize perseverance and glory.

Knowst thou the land where the lemon trees bloom,
Where the gold orange glows in the deep
   thicket's gloom,
Where a wind ever soft from the blue
   heaven blows,
And the groves are of laurel and myrtle and rose?

—Johann Wolfgang von Goethe,
Wilhelm Meister's Apprenticeship

tion they may also have shared with their new white neighbors.

❧

Though the medicinal virtues of these leaves have waned, they are still used sparingly for cooking to flavor soups, stews, and puddings. An Englishman visiting the United States was heard to declare that he would no more put them in his soup than he would gasoline.

We'll go to the woods no more,
The laurels are all cut.

—A. E. Housman, Last Poems

California Laurel

CAMPHOR TREE

Camphor Tree   *Cinnamomum camphora*   (Laurel Tree)

rush a leaf from the camphor tree, and the strong, clean scent of mothballs rises to your nose. This is the tree whose leaves, bark, and wood were the original source of commercial camphor, a substance whose sharp, penetrating odor repels moths. The pungent gum that rids your closet of destructive insects has also had more urgent uses—specifically, in medicine.

Because native camphor trees were so highly valued for healing in old China, the penalty for cutting one down was death. There, called by the harmonious name of *Hsiang chang*, camphor was an important medicinal for cardiac and circulatory disorders and also a tonifying remedy for the stomach and the entire digestive system. Even today, Chinese herbal doctors recommend it for the same illnesses.

Western doctors used to prescribe camphor as a nerve sedative, for calming the symptoms of convulsions, hysteria, insomnia, and general nervousness. In small doses, it was believed beneficial as a stimulant of the respiratory organs as well as for treating heavy colds, severe catarrhal conditions, and asthma. An oil treated with camphor, and called

> he thick old Camphor trees across the street…they said the trees were planted as protection against fever, that if you had a Camphor tree outside your house…you didn't get Yellow Fever.
>
> —Shirley Ann Grau,
> The House on Coliseum Street

"camphorated oil" used internally and externally, benefited diarrhea and rheumatism and other muscular pains.

In Europe today, as in old China, camphor is considered a valuable heart stimulant, especially useful for stopping cardiac fibrillation, though American physicians disagree about these claims. Though camphor is now synthetically produced, the molecular or chemical formula used is based on the makeup of the natural substance once extracted from the leaves and wood of the camphor tree.

For now these handsome trees bearing fragrant, evergreen leaves are mainly relied upon to provide beauty and deep, cooling shade to the streets of California, Florida, and other warm, sunny states of America.

Camphor

CAPER BUSH

Caper Bush   *Capparis spinosa*   (Caper Family)

A straggling shrub on a rocky perch, the caper bush clings tenaciously to life by thrusting its invasive roots to the cracks and crevices of rocks and stone walls. Its large, stunning blossoms, white or violet with lavender stamens in the center, look strangely out of place, even outshining the modest trailing shrub that bears them. The small, immature flower bud from which this splendid flower develops and eventually blooms is the flavorsome green condiment known simply as the caper.

❦

These piquant young buds are patiently gathered by hand—one by one—then pickled in vinegar or preserved in dry salt or brine. Capers are used to enliven salads, pasta sauces, meat, fish, and a variety of other savory dishes, especially in Mediterranean cuisines.

❦

Though the small, green flower buds are the plant part most commonly used as a condiment, the round, evergreen leaves are sometimes preserved— such as on the Mediterranean island of Cyprus—for the same purpose.

❦

In southern Italy and Greece, caper leaves were once considered an effective diuretic, astringent, and tonic, though their therapeutic use was only occasional and slight.

❦

Perhaps the most interesting characteristic of these disklike leaves is observed

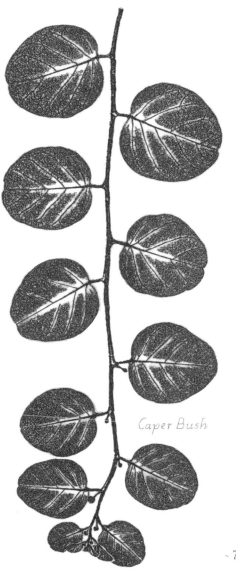

Caper Bush

when the shrub grows in hot, dry climates, such as in the African Sahara. During the hottest, driest part of the day, the leaves turn themselves edgewise to the sun, allowing them to avoid extreme dehydration and protecting the very life of the plant. Clinging to the arid desert rocks, the rambling caper bush relies upon the scant vapor of the desert air to maintain itself fresh and green.

Once, for example, when I was just starting out in the food business, I was hired by the caper people to develop a lot of recipes using capers, and it was weeks of tossing capers into just about everything but milkshakes before I came to terms with the fact that nobody really likes capers no matter what you do with them. Some people pretend to like capers, but the truth is that any dish that tastes good with capers in it tastes even better with capers not in it.

—Nora Ephron, Heartburn

Castor Oil Shrub

CASTOR OIL PLANT

Castor Oil Plant and Shrub   *Ricinus communis*   (Spurge Family)

The large, elegant leaf extended like a hand to heal and bless gives this plant an appropriately descriptive name, palma christi—hand of Christ—a double reference to its benevolent, medicinal virtue and to the shape of its leaves. Castor oil shrub is, however, the more familiar name for this plant whose crushed seeds are the source of a valuable oil that is put to both therapeutic and industrial uses. The seeds, from their resemblance to a dog tick, give it the scientific name *Ricinus*, which in Latin means "tick."

Since the seeds themselves are deadly poison—one to three are fatal to children—it follows that the oil pressed from them is also toxic. A noxious protein, ricin, lurks within, but by crushing the seeds between rollers at a temperature not over fifty degrees the oil extracted becomes medically safe as an effective purgative. The powerful action and nauseous taste of this oil have caused generations of children to weep at the mere mention of a possible dose. Mussolini, one of the most ruthless dictators of modern times, administered massive quantities of this oil as a violent punishment to imprisoned enemies.

While most healing uses of this plant come from the oil, the recorded uses of the leaves, though less commonly known, go back two thousand years. Chinese medicine, calling this plant *Pi ma*, prescribed solutions from these leaves for disorders of the stomach and digestive tract.

※

Dioscorides, the famous Greek physician of the first century, recommended the castor oil plant as a medicinal, saying, "Ye leaves being bruised with the flour of Polenta [ground meal], doe assuage Oedemata [swellings] and inflammations of ye eyes, and do abate milk and swollen breasts, and extinguisheth Erysipelata, [infected inflammations], when laid on by itself, or with Acetum [vinegar]."

※

While these poisonous leaves are never used for human food, insects relish them. In Asia, they

are greedily eaten by Tussah silkworms, and in

Some believe that castor oil can help fade stretchmarks and advise an external application of it two to three times daily during and after pregnancy.

India by Eri silkmoths. People claim that when caterpillars are nourished on castor leaves, the silk they produce, though rough, is endlessly durable.

※

This plant is a striking embellishment in American gardens thanks to its large, luxuriant leaves and, in the dark red varieties, its attractive color. Because of its size it is best used in large gardens, where it serves as a tall, leafy screen. In areas where it is warm year-round, such as Africa, it develops into a woody shrub, even an ornamental small tree.

> The hand of a leaf
> Splitting and sifting the air—
> The blueness of breath.
>
> —Ann Atwood, The Mood of Earth

CATALPA

Catalpa   *Catalpa bignoniodes*   (Bignonia Family)

The Cherokees called this tree *kutuhlpa*, which is not far from its present common name of catalpa. Native to the Gulf Coast of the southern United States, it has also been planted as an ornamental in the north. Today, flourishing vigorously outside of its original area, it has even escaped into the wild from New England to Michigan.

Among the catalpa's unique distinctions are its large heart-shaped leaves and rich clusters of spotted white-and-gold blossoms; even more interesting are the long, pendant, pencil-form seedpods that resemble string beans. Growing from between nine to twelve inches long and remaining on the tree throughout the winter, they are responsible for the catalpa's other known name of bean tree. But when winter-bare, except for the slender pods, the catalpa is unexceptional—even uninteresting

The catalpa, to the casual observer, looks confusingly like another tree, the paulownia, which often grows in the same parts of the United States. This look-alike, originally from China, has similar large but sometimes variable leaves—heart-shaped or slightly lobed. However, when the paulownia puts forth its distinguishing bouquets of fragrant, violet flowers, and later, its clustered, upright, and woody seed capsules, the similarity ceases. The flowers and seedpods of each tree declare its true identity.

Native Americans of the Gulf Coast and early settlers concocted minor herbal remedies from the catalpa's leaves.

Though these leaves, when bruised, emit an extremely unpleasant, even noxious, odor, they still applied them, crushed and beaten as poultices, on wounds to the skin. For an internal medicine, they combined equal parts of the leaves and the thin, fresh inner bark to make a tincture with a mild cathartic action. Except when taken in very large doses, this gentle but most unpleasant-tasting remedy was said to be only moderately effective.

Green catalpa leaves and a green-and-black caterpillar have joined to give fame and another name to this tree. The three-inch-long larva of a hummingbird-like moth, the catalpa sphinx, finds the leaves of this tree satisfying and delicious and, as the tree's most serious pest, sometimes even completely defoliates it. Calling them catawba-worms (from catawba, a colloquial term for catalpa), fishermen gather these larvae from the trees and use them as a bait that fish find irresistible. And from this, the tree is locally known as fish-bait tree in the Gulf Coast south.

Catalpa wood is slightly aromatic, soft, and somewhat weak, yet possesses a lasting quality. It is a popular wood used most often for fence posts and decorative items such as picture frames.

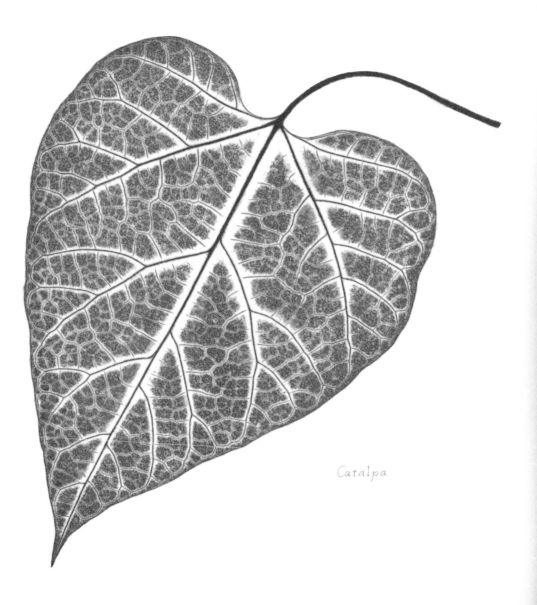

Catalpa

CECROPIA TREE

Cecropia Tree   *Cecropia palmata*   (Mulberry)

Neither graceful, nor beautiful, nor the bearer of bright flowers or sweet fruit, the awkward but benevolent cecropia tree protects, shelters, and nourishes life.

❧

People living in the cecropia's Caribbean homeland say it protects by showing the silver undersides of its wind-tossed leaves when a hurricane is approaching. It shelters in its hollow stems hordes of fierce, biting Azteca ants that suddenly rush out to defend their homes and young when the tree is disturbed. And for one lethargic animal, the three-toed sloth, the leaves of the cecropia tree are a primary source of nourishment.

❧

This sloth, while hooking its claws over a branch, spends its rather long but mostly uneventful life hanging upside down in this tropical tree. So rarely does it leave the tree that during damp weather, green algae forms on its fur, giving it a protective coloration amid the green leaves.

❧

These idle animals sleep ten to twenty hours a day, but even when fully awake, they seem to peer at the world through sleepy eyes while peacefully pursuing their almost sole activity: filling their disproportionately large stomachs with leaves, usually those of the cecropia tree.

❧

Zoologists once thought that the three-toed sloth ate cecropia leaves exclusively, scorning all others. However, it has been shown that while cecropia leaves are often preferred, these sloths may eat other varieties of foliage. Still, a sloth with a distinct preference for cecropia cannot survive for long in an environment, such as a northern zoo, that lacks an abundant supply.

✤

According to the latest zoological discoveries, arboreal creatures eating exclusively the leaves of the trees they inhabit have lower metabolic rates than grass-eaters or fruit-eaters of the same size, and this slower metabolism results in reduced activity. The leafy cecropia diet is, thus, the cause of the sloth's markedly placid behavior.

Note: The young leaf in this illustration is much smaller and has a shorter stem than a mature cecropia leaf.

Cecropia

Red Cedar

He went down
As when a lordly cedar,
    green with boughs,
Goes down with a great
    shout upon the hills
And leaves a lonesome place
    against the sky.

    —Edwin Markham
The Man with the Hoe

Note: The print shows both
the mature and the needled
juvenile foliage.

RED CEDAR

Red Cedar   *Juniperus virginiana*   (Cypress Family)

f all the names in the verdant world of trees, cedar is one of the most ambiguous and confusing. While there are trees to which this name rightfully belongs—the atlas cedars of North Africa, the deodar cedars of India, and the Lebanon cedars of the Near East—the American tree illustrated here, though called a cedar, is botanically different and does not truly deserve the title. The tree pictured here is really a juniper, but for popular recognition, in this book it is still called red cedar. A quick definitive guide for identification explains, "Junipers have berries—Cedars have cones."

❧

This dense, columnar tree grows in almost any soil, thriving even under unfavorable conditions—on dry hills, in abandoned fields, in hedgerows, and along roadsides—across the eastern half of the United States, extending also into Minnesota, North Dakota, Texas, and sometimes beyond. The foliage, the wood, and the blue berries are all intensely aromatic; even more, they are healing.

❧

For Native Americans this tree was once a green and living pharmacy. The volatile oil distilled from the leaves and berries relieved the symptoms of rheumatism; boiled leaves eased bronchitis in humans and horses; bruised leaves and berries cured headaches; the vapor of boiling leaves inhaled through the open mouth dulled agonizing toothaches; and decoctions of boiled leaves strengthened the weak, helped the convalescent, facilitated childbirth, cured dysentery, and banished worms in children.

❧

One specific instance of the Native American use of cedar is legendary. During the winter of 1849–50, an epidemic of Asiatic cholera broke out among the Dakota Indians, decimating their numbers and causing many to flee. The tribe's young chief, Red Cloud, tried every remedy for his people that his desperate medicine men could devise.

❧

Finally, a cure was effected using a successful combination of a hot decoction of cedar foliage taken internally, and an external medicinal bath.

❧

Even the authoritative *U.S. Pharmacopoeia* recognized cedar's therapeutic worth, including it from 1820 through 1894 among its listings of healing medicines.

❧

Cedar is still valuable today, but in other ways. Cedar chests and closets discourage moths and impart a clean fragrance to stored clothes, while the aromatic oil from both leaves and wood is used in perfumes. In the wild, winter-hungry deer browse on the evergreen foliage, and uncounted thousands of birds eagerly strip the blue berries from the branches.

❧

As their name reveals, cedar wax-wings are especially fond of berries. Robert Penn Warren wrote in a poem, "The wax-wing's beak slices the blue cedarberry which is as blue as distance."

CHASTE TREE

Chaste Tree *Vitex agnus-castus* (Vervain Family)

In ancient Greece, because the leaves of this tree were known to be peculiarly sedative, they were vital to the rites annually held in honor of the goddess of harvests. Celebrated chiefly by women, the purpose of this festival was to ensure the fertility of the fields; however, during the ceremonies the celebrants themselves were supposed to remain pure and chaste.

✿

In the words of the Roman naturalist Pliny, "There is a kind of tree named Vitex [and], during the feasts of the goddess Ceres which were named the Thesmorphia...the dames of Athens...made their pallets and beds with the leaves thereof to cool the heat of lust, and to keep themselves chaste for the time."

✿

It was not only Pliny who knew the reputation of this tree and its leaves, but Dioscorides, the ancient Greek physician, too, as well as later herbalists of other countries. From the ancient use of its soothing leaves, vitex gets its common name, chaste tree.

✿

According to old herbal medicine, these aromatic leaves had certain beneficent powers other than the cooling of lust. A simple sprig of leaves carried on the person reputedly drove away all "venomous beasts," including serpents, while a poultice of the leaves cured their poisonous bite. A decoction of these leaves and seeds together was once thought good for curing all "griefs and inflammations of the womb," healing "disjointures and wounds," dissolving swellings, and dispelling "headache and lethargy."

✸

In America today the once-therapeutic chaste tree is valued neither for its sedative nor its healing qualities. Instead, it is now appreciated as a flowering ornament for embellishing summer gardens. Anxious gardeners, noting its lack of greenery and blossom in early springtime, are rewarded weeks later when it belatedly puts forth its gray-green, fingered leaves and its ample spikes of violet bloom.

✸

Chaste Tree

CHERRY LAUREL

Cherry Laurel   *Prunus laurocerasus*   (Rose Family)

In 1781 a man was hanged in Rugby, England, because of the lovely but lethal leaves of the cherry laurel, a decorative shrub.

❦

Four years earlier Captain John Donellan, an unscrupulous retired army officer, hoping to better his own financial position, had married Theodosia Boughton, a titled English lady who shared a comfortable fortune with her brother, Sir Theodosius Boughton. Because Sir Theo was sickly, frequently taking medicine, Captain Donellan devised an evil but appropriate scheme for eliminating him, thus hoping to increase his wife's share of the inheritance, and also knowing that as lord of the manor, he would be able to spend her fortune. By substituting a potion he had concocted from poisonous cherry laurel leaves for the medicine recently sent to Sir Theo by a local pharmacist, Donellan set the stage for his sinister plan.

❦

On August 30, 1780, when Sir Theo's mother gave her son his medicine, she noticed both an unusual sediment and a nauseating odor. Thinking it merely a new prescription, she urged her son to swallow it. Almost immediately, Sir Theo went into convulsions, and minutes later he died. On being called, Captain Donellan tasted a drop; then, over his mother-in-

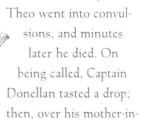

law's protests, he emptied the remaining medicine into a basin.

※

Sir Theo was buried without an inquest, but when rumors began circulating and suspicions mounted, legal procedures were initiated. After a coroner's jury brought in a verdict of willful murder against Captain Donellan, a trial date was set for March 30, 1781.

※

During the brief trial, it was revealed that a book describing the deadly effects of cherry laurel water was found in Donellan's possession, with the page where the directions for its preparation appeared doubled over. Admitting acquaintance with laurel water, Donellan claimed he used it in a foot-bath after an attack of gout, or sometimes to kill fleas.

※

Donellan was found guilty of murder and condemned to death. In pronouncing the sentence, the judge declared, "Avarice was the motive, and hypocrisy the instrument and veil." Before dying, while still self-righteously maintaining his innocence, Donellan said, "I solemnly swear that I am innocent of the crime for which I suffer. I hope the world will believe the last words of a dying man who here falls victim to the black devices of a mother-in-law." (She had, of course, testified against him.) The sentence was swiftly carried out, and on April 1, 1781, Captain Donellan was hanged by the neck until dead.

Oh, talk not to me of a name great in story,
The days of our youth are the days of
*   our glory;*
And the myrtle and ivy of sweet
*   two-and-twenty*
Are worth all your laurels, though
*   ever so plenty.*

— Lord Byron

Cherry Laurel

SWEET CHERRY

Sweet Cherry Tree   *Prunus avium*   (Rose Family)

"If you want to know what cherries taste like," said the German poet Goethe, "you must ask birds and boys." And those who have a cherry tree in the garden know this is true. Its juicy, small, but delicious fruit is, of course, the ultimate reason for the tree's cultivation.

✦

As early as 65 B.C., Lucullus, an ancient gourmet and Roman consul, is said to have introduced this tree of Eurasian origin into Italy, where it has flourished ever since. Many years later, the English colonists brought it to America.

✦

The tree itself, wondrous within and without, is a delight in all seasons: in spring blossom a cloud of white; in summer hung with fruit—red, sometimes golden; and year-round boasting a beautiful display of birchlike red-brown bark. Its wood, one of the most handsome in color and grain, is prized for fine furniture. And the sticky gum exuding from a wound on the tree's surface was once considered medically valuable. As for the dark, lovely leaves, there is one former use that gives them a special importance. In the following Old World recipe, cherry leaves lend their unique flavor to cucumber-pickle brine.

✦

For twenty-five, six-inch cucumbers, two quarts of leaves are needed. Place the washed cucumbers in a large crock in alternating layers with the leaves, scattering over everything a quarter cup of caraway seeds. Cover this completely with a strong brine solution—a half cup of salt to a gallon of water. Place a weighted plate on top to keep everything under the liquid, and allow this to remain undisturbed for fourteen days. At the end of that time, discard the leaves, drain the pickles for an hour, and, after cutting them into one-inch chunks, pack them into sterilized quart jars. Boil three pounds of sugar with a pint of vinegar and a quarter cup of mixed pickling-spice until the sugar is dissolved. Pour this boiling syrup over the pickles, then seal immediately.

The end of spring
lingers
    in the cherry blossoms.
—Haiku by Yosa Buson
(1716–1783)

Sweet Cherry

WILD BLACK CHERRY

Wild Black-Cherry Tree   *Prunus serotina*   (Rose Family)

Like the sweet cherry, the wild black cherry tree of the eastern United States is haunted by birds, small animals, and especially small children. The fruit it bears, neither as large nor delicious as sweet cherries, has instead an odd, bittersweet flavor. Even more alluring to children, the clustered fruits while still small, green, and hard make handy ammunition for country urchins. Because of this, countless millions of green cherries, especially those on branches overhanging sidewalks, never live to ripen until black.

※

People with more mature tastes find a special use for well-ripened wild black cherries; they are excellent

New England Indians would preserve cherries by pounding them, stones and all, between flat stones, then drying them on pieces of birch bark.

for adding flavor and color to whiskey. To make this country liquor, fill a bottle with ripe cherries, the skin of each pierced with a needle; pour in the whiskey, seal, and allow to stand for a month before drinking.

※

The wood of this tree, the largest of the rose family native to North America, is smooth-grained and handsome, perfect for furniture and fine interior paneling. Because it never shrinks, cherry wood is also sought

Wild Black Cherry

Loveliest of trees, the cherry now
Is hung with bloom along the bough.

—A. E. Housman
A Shropshire Lad

So we grew together,
Like to a double cherry, seeming parted,
But yet a union in partition;
Two lovely berries moulded on one stem;
So, with two seeming bodies, but one heart.

—William Shakespeare,
A Midsummer Night's Dream

for making spirit levels, a device used for ascertaining a true horizontal line.

✳

Of all species of native cherries in the eastern United States, including the pin cherry and the choke-cherry, the foliage of the wild black cherry is the most dangerous to live-stock. When its branches are cut from the tree, the withered leaves develop hydrocyanic (prussic) acid, a potent poison, that possesses the pleasant odor of bitter almonds. Fresh or thoroughly dried leaves are relatively harmless, but when animals feed on large amounts of wilted leaves, the brain, heart, and lungs are rapidly damaged, causing staggering and convulsions, inevitably followed by death within an hour. Fortunately, cattle and sheep will not seek black cherry foliage when more palatable forage is abundant.

✳

The leaves of this tree are a favorite food of the tent caterpillar, which sometimes attacks in such overwhelming numbers that all of the branches are totally defoliated. The tree, however, displays an amazing vitality. One naturalist reported seeing a wild cherry tree completely stripped of its leaves in mid-May, then miraculously recovered a few weeks later.

To relieve discomfort from measles, drink tea
made from the bark of the wild black-cherry tree.

AMERICAN CHESTNUT

American Chestnut   *Castanea dentata*   (Beech Family)

The chestnut tree, high, wide, and handsome, once a familiar sight and an abundant presence in American forests, is now only a fading memory. Where stout branches once upheld great canopies of leaves, there are now only gray, leafless skeletons. In less than one human generation, this once-dominant tree was completely eliminated by the deadly chestnut blight of Asiatic origin, a fungal bark disease spread by windblown spores. This disease, first recognized in 1904 in a New York City park, raged in all directions like a firestorm.

Today young shoots still grow from old roots, flowering and sometimes even bearing nuts. After a few years, however, these struggling, young trees are, in turn, killed by the fatal blight. Dendrologists still watch and hope for a resistant strain from which resurgent forests may one day rise.

In an attempt to fill the gap, Japanese and Chinese chestnut species have been introduced and so far have not fallen victim to the dread disease. However, these Asian trees are smaller, less splendid specimens, and the nuts they bear are also smaller, less abundant, and, some say, less flavorful. Attempts are being made to create disease-resistant hybrids by crossing the American with the Asian species, but with only limited success thus far.

※

Before this American botanical tragedy occurred, the leaves of the native chestnut had practical uses in folk and also scientific medicine. Native Americans drank a tea made with the leaves as a remedy for coughs. The early colonists also concocted a medicinal tea, which when mixed with honey was a soothing cough syrup.

The chestnut tree made famous in Longfellow's poem "The Village Blacksmith" was a real tree in Cambridge. It was unfortunately cut down to make way for a larger road, but some of its wood was fashioned into a chair and presented to Longfellow on his ninety-second birthday.

Even in those medically primitive times, the extract from leaves was understood to have a sedative effect on the respiratory nerves.

※

Later, country folk used the leaves to make astringent poultices for burns, and with the juice of the leaves they quelled the unbearable itching of skin rashes such as poison ivy. Ingenious and frugal, they also found another practical use. They filled their mattresses with dry chestnut leaves, which, because they rustled when lain upon, were humorously known as talking beds.

※

Between 1873 and 1905 chestnut leaves, known to pharmacologists as *extractum castanea fluidum*, were considered so valuable that they were included in the prestigious *U.S. Pharmacopoeia*.

American
Chestnut

The chestnut casts his flambeaux, and the flowers
  Stream the hawthorn on the wind away,
The doors clap to, the pane is blind with showers.
  Pass the can, lad; there's an end to May.

—A. E. Housman, Lancer

CHINABERRY

Chinaberry Tree   *Melia azedarach*   (Mahogany Family)

The phoenix and the unicorn eat the fruits of the chinaberry tree, but dragons abhor them, at least according to an ancient Chinese myth. If this tale is true, then these fabled beasts are the only creatures who can safely eat the yellow chinaberries, since for all others they are highly toxic, causing intestinal inflammation, paralysis, even death.

It is not only the berries that are dangerous but all other parts of this tree. The pale lavender flowers, bark, roots, and large, lacy leaves all contain toxic poisons whose narcotic action attacks the central nervous system. Pierandrea Mattioli, a sixteenth-century Italian physician, wrote, "It bringeth death even unto beasts."

But chinaberry leaves, like those of other poisonous plants, have had good uses as well as evil ones. When appropriately prepared and properly used, the leaves are effective in insecticide sprays; they repel moths in stored clothing and also deter insects from invading dried beans and fruits. Country folk once placed these leaves under mattresses to eliminate fleas and lice. Rubbed onto the skin, they relieved fungal skin disorders. And carefully controlled infusions of the leaves taken inwardly drive out intestinal worms, though this is considered a dangerous antidote because an overdose can kill.

The chinaberry tree, native to Asia, was brought to Europe in the seventeenth century where, according to reliable records, it was known to be in cultivation. In addition, it was reportedly growing in England in 1656. François André Michaux, a French botanist who traveled in colonial America observing native plants, is credited with introducing it into Charleston, South Carolina, in the 1790s. Since that time it has prospered and flourished, shading countless southern dooryards with its large, intricate leaves.

❧

The graceful leaves, the airy panicles of lavender flowers, and the clustered golden berries all combine to make this Asian wanderer one of our loveliest imports. Though originally planted in colonial gardens, the chinaberry tree has adapted so well to American soil and climate that it has now spread into the wild, mingling freely with the native trees of the American South.

❧

Chinaberry

Citrus Trees

In the full of spring on the banks of a river
Two big gardens planted with thousands of Orange trees
Their thick leaves putting the clouds to shame.

—Tu Fu, Chinese poet (A.D. 712–770)

CITRUS TREES

Citrus Trees   *Citrus species*   (Rue Family)

Try to imagine a world without oranges, lemons, limes, or grapefruits, without orange marmalade, lemon meringue pie, or orange blossom cocktails—the grim list goes on and on. And quite the worst, contemplate a long, hot summer without ice-cold lemonade. For Americans accustomed to bountiful, daily supplies of these fruits from Florida, California, and other warm states, life without citrus is unthinkable.

❦

The handsome, fragrant, and useful trees that bear these fruits originally came from Asia. From there they have spread into all the warm regions of the world, where they have been abundantly cultivated for centuries. The very similar leathery leaves of these trees all contain an essential oil that releases a lemony odor when the leaves are crushed in the hand.

❦

In Europe, perfume makers in particular depend heavily on citrus leaves, distilling them with their fresh green twigs to make *petit-grain*, a vital essence for enhancing alluring fragrances.

❦

Country folk in the Caribbean scent their baths with lemon leaves and also use them in an after-shampoo hair rinse.

The royal ladies of King Louis XIV's court would bite into lemons to redden their lips.

In Mexico a soothing decoction of orange leaves coaxes peaceful slumber, while lime leaves in tea with honey calm the irritation of a cold.

⁂

The imaginative people of southern Italy once believed a lemon-leaf crown was an effective cure for headaches, while today they wrap the leaves around mozzarella cheese before grilling it, which imparts the cheese with a special aroma.

⁂

A common American folklore remedy for curing a cold was to drink hot lemonade made with whole lemons, rind and all.

In the celebrated Mediterranean town of Sorrento lemon leaves are used to make a popular sweet called fornarini. Very ripe white grapes are sprinkled with sugar and grated lemon peel and then completely enclosed in lemon leaves, which are then tied shut with a strong strand of grass. The small green packages are baked slowly until the leaves are crisply dry, then removed from the oven and opened to reveal sweet, juicy, lemon-scented raisins.

COCA

Coca   *Erhtbroxylum coca*   (Coca Family)

riginating in South America, coca, the "divine plant of the Incas," has been known, used, and abused for thousands of years—in religion, to communicate with the spirits; in medicine, to lighten labor; as a stimulant or euphoriant; and as an illegal social drug.

❧

Coca thrives on the high, moist, eastern slope of the Andes in Bolivia, Columbia, Peru, and Argentina. Picked by women and children, the leaves are an abundant crop, yielding over two thousand pounds per acre. Coca chewers in South America consume much of this harvest, and the rest is exported legally and illegally.

❧

For over three thousand years in South America, coca leaves chewed with lime—sometimes from powdered seashells—to activate their narcotic substances have banished pain and given strength to the Indians. Today, too, Indian males, beginning around the age of eight and continuing throughout their lives, chew about two ounces of leaves daily.

❧

Centuries before cocaine was known to modern medicine, the early Incas were using these pain-dulling leaves—although primitively—in surgery for amputating limbs, excising tumors, and performing cesarean sections.

❧

Even now in South American folk medicine, these leaves are used therapeutically for gastric disturbances, altitude sickness, rheumatism, and malaria.

*

The use in modern medicine of cocaine extracted from these leaves began in 1884, when a young Austrian surgeon, Karl Koller, used it during eye operations. Soon its use spread to surgery in rhinology, laryngology, urology, and dentistry. Today it is still principally employed for operations of the nose and throat, while in an ointment it relieves painful skin diseases; given internally, it mitigates the pain of cancer.

*

Concerned nations have exerted great effort to control the use of cocaine as a social drug but with little success; instead its use continues to spread.

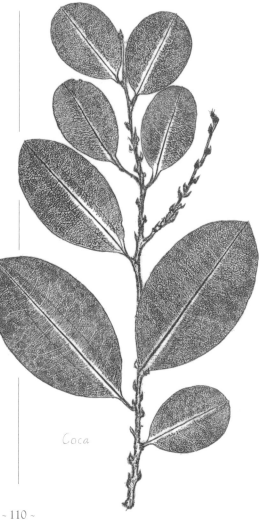

Coca

ARIZONA CYPRESS

Arizona Cypress   *Cupressus arizonica*   (Cypress Family)

An elegant, silvery Christmas tree, a source of Native American herbal medicine, and an exotic ornament in foreign parks—these are the various uses of the Arizona cypress.

❋

This pale, blue-green tree is native to the mountains of the arid American Southwest. The small leaves are actually green, but they are covered by a protective bluish wax that prevents the water the tree needs for survival from evaporating in its parched environment.

❋

In 1917, after the Union of South Africa ordered forty pounds of Arizona cypress seeds, requests for more seeds began to arrive from dry-weather countries all over the world. Today more prevalent abroad than in the United States, this tree continues to be appreciated for its ability to thrive in difficult climates and also to prevent erosion. It is also especially handsome when planted near trees with maroon leaves, where its unique frosty color creates a striking contrast.

❋

At home in its native American Southwest, this cypress is popular as a Christmas tree not only for its compact bushy form and its cool silver hue but also because it is unusually long-lasting indoors, thanks again to the waxy coating on its foliage, which keeps it from drying out.

❋

This native tree was once important to the Native Americans of the Southwest as a source of effective medicine. They believed the vapor of the burning leaves was helpful for removing afterbirth, for shrinking the womb, and also for increasing the flow of urine. They pounded the living leaves into a disinfecting poultice effective for treating ringworm and other fungoid diseases. And to relieve the agony of toothaches, for healing ulcers, and reducing tumors, they applied compresses of crushed leaves. In addition, the resinous odor of cypress fumigated and sweetened the air in their homes.

❧

The green medicine of the cypress is now long gone and all but forgotten, but this misty, silver-blue tree still continues to flourish in the parched areas of the Southwest. And though the Arizona cypress is a true native American, it is oddly enough a more frequent presence in foreign parks and public gardens than it is here in its own United States.

Arizona Cypress

ITALIAN CYPRESS

Italian Cypress *Cupressus sempervirens* (Cypress Family)

Anyone who has seen the enchanted landscape of southern Italy has surely noticed the cypresses. Tall, black-green, and spirelike, they rise like living exclamation points emphatically punctuating the countryside.

❧

These evergreen trees native to the Himalaya of western Asia are thought to have been introduced into the Middle East and also southern Europe by the seafaring Phoenicians a thousand years before Christ. The classical authors of Greece and Rome mentioned the cypress in their ancient writings.

❧

The olden Persians regarded the cypress—always green—as the symbol of eternal life. But in Rome, mourners in funeral processions carried branches of cypress or wore cypress wreaths to express the irrevocability of death, an idea arising from an old conviction that

the living tree, once cut, would never grow again. All over Italy, cypress trees and death have always had close ties, and even today, tall, dark cypresses stand like solemn sentinels in countless Italian cemeteries.

❧

Cypress was important in early medicine. Dioscorides, a first-century Greek physician to the Roman army, discussed it in his remarkable work, *De Materia*

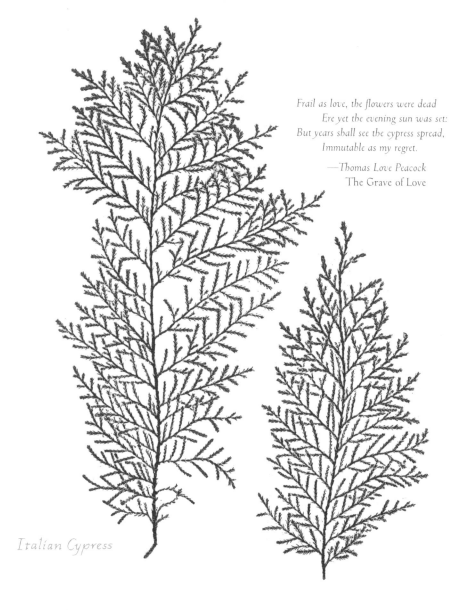

Frail as love, the flowers were dead
Ere yet the evening sun was set:
But years shall see the cypress spread,
Immutable as my regret.

—*Thomas Love Peacock*
The Grave of Love

Italian Cypress

Medica, in which he credited the leaves, when combined with drink, with many healing virtues, including strengthening the stomach, aiding the gallbladder, and as a poultice, closing up wounds and stanching the flow of blood. He further maintained that it cured carbuncles and banished erysipelas, herpes, and inflammations of the eyes.

❦

In the same century, the Roman naturalist Pliny confidently listed still other benefits, claiming it effective for sunstroke, hernia, swollen testicles, and poisonous spider bites. And finally, applied with vinegar, he said it dyed the hair black.

❦

In the sixteenth century the English botanist John Gerard endorsed some of these wonder cures and also added others. "Cypress," he wrote, "takes away the Polypus, being an excrescence growing in the nose," and "the leaves boyled

Cypress essential oil has high astringent properties and appears to aid somewhat in the treatment of varicose veins. Mix a few drops of it into a neutral cream or some mineral oil and apply daily to affected legs using a gentle upward motion.

with sweet wine helps the strangurie and difficulty of making water." Ending with a final flourish, he declared, "It doth drive away gnats."

❦

Contrary to its former abounding medicinal power, today the sole recognized value of the essential oil is its effectiveness as a soothing inhalant, a reliable specific in whooping cough.

❦

And as they have done for a thousand years, cypress trees continue to guard the dreamless sleep of the Italian dead.

❦

Like late snow
After winter is ended
Flakes falling, caught and held
In some unearthly swirl.

—John Gould Fletcher
South Star

Flowering Dogwood

FLOWERING DOGWOOD

Flowering Dogwood   *Cornus florida*   (Dogwood Family)

As botanists always hasten to point out, the white-petalled dogwood "flowers" are really not flowers at all. Botanically speaking, the so-called white petals are "bracts," modified leaves that surround the small, central, knobby green structures, the true flowers. But whatever their name, bracts or petals, the springtime woodlands of eastern North America are gloriously illuminated by their shining whiteness. Occasionally, wild dogwood grows in shades of pink; named horticultural varieties are available from nurseries in this attractive color.

In fall, too, dogwood lights the woods of the dying year with the crimson of its autumn foliage. The small fruits also shine scarlet while providing a feast for the many varieties of seed-eating birds that hungrily strip the berries from the branches.

Sam Ragan, a poet of North Carolina, where the dogwood is a state symbol, has lyrically observed this seasonal change of color:

> From Dogwood white to Dogwood red,
> That's the way the summer's fled.

The Native Americans found practical

uses for dogwood in their herbal medicine, discovering certain modest therapeutic benefits. For intermittent or malarial type fevers, they infused a combination of the white floral bracts, the green, true leaves, and the pale inner bark of this tree. This same mixture in a weaker tea was given to infants suffering from flatulent colic.

※

The provocative name "dogwood" always arouses questions about its possible origin, queries that have elicited an interesting variety of answers. Some claim it is so called because a decoction of the bark from another species of dogwood *(Cornus sanquinea)* was formerly used in England as a healing wash for mangy dogs. Another tentative explana‑ tion supposes that his tree may once have been called not "dogwood" but "dagwood," short for "daggerwood," a name implying that this hard, dense and tough wood was once used for weapons, or perhaps at least for skewers. And finally, a third possibility—but the least likely of all—suggests that this name is an anagram formed from the inverted letters of "godwood," a reference to the improbable idea that Christ may have been crucified on a cross of this wood. All of these tenuous explanations are merely imaginative, unconfirmed speculations.

※

As the ultimate tribute to this beauteous tree, near the end of his life, Irvin S. Cobb, the Kentucky humorist, said: "Lay my ashes at the foot of a dogwood tree—should the tree live, that will be monument enough for me."

※

DUTCHMAN'S PIPE

Dutchman's Pipe *Aristolochia durior* (Birthwort Family)

The ample green hearts covering arbors and trellises and shading many American porches are the handsome leaves of a wild vine that has been introduced into cultivation. Dutchman's pipe is native to the fertile forests of eastern North America from New England south to Alabama; only rarely does it grow in the wild as far west as Minnesota. This high climber owes its name to its brownish purple flowers, which are shaped and curved like old Dutch tobacco pipes.

Its scientific name, *Aristolochia*, however, is more revealing. Dioscorides named this entire plant group by combining two Greek words—*aristos* (best) and *locheia* (childbirth)—a clue to its ancient use. One of its English names is birthwort; "wort" is an old Anglo-Saxon word for plant.

Since Greco-Roman time, plants of this same group have been used against cancer, and research at the University of Wisconsin corroborates this ancient wisdom. There, in laboratory investigations, a substance called aristolochic acid, extracted from the leaves of Dutchman's pipe, has been found to exhibit cancer-fighting activity. And, like many other plants containing important medicinal properties, this one and all of the members of its family are dangerously poisonous. It is not toxic, however, when casually touched—only when ingested.

Dutchman's Pipe

ELDERBERRY

American Elderberry   *Sambucus canadensis*   (Honeysuckle Family)

gnore the elderberry shrub at your own peril—if old doctors and early herbalists are still to be believed. Flourishing near ditches and swamps, this common shrub, a familiar plant in North America, as well as its close European relatives, was once regarded with superstitious respect and seriously sought for almost endless medical cures.

✻

Dr. Hermann Boerhaave, a seventeenth-century Dutch physician, addressed it thus: "Elder, elder, may I pluck your branches? If no rebuke follows," he said,

For an effective skin wash good for minor scrapes, stings, and sunburn, simmer 1 cup of dried leaves in 2 cups of water for 10 minutes. Apply as needed.

"one should spit three times and then proceed," adding, "It deserves the respect of men for its many 'Galenical,' salubrious uses." (Galen was a famous second-century Greek physician.)

✻

In 1664, English nature writer John Evelyn declared, "If the medicinal properties of its leaves, bark and berries were fully known, I cannot tell what our country-man could ail for which he might not fetch a remedy from every hedge for sickness and wounds." Another enthusiastic naturalist maintained: "In domestic medicine, this plant forms almost a complete pharmacy in itself."

✻

Among their many healing virtues, elder leaves were regarded as a purga-

Elderberry

tive. In 1633 John Gerard, the celebrated English herbalist noted, "The leaves of common elder open the belly, purging both slimy flegme and chlolericke humors." Another folk healer promised this mysterious cure: "The juice of green Elder leaves, sniffed up the nostrils, purges the tunicles of the brain."

The recital of its wonders continues: inflammation of the eyes, headaches, fungus infections, eczema, sprains, bruises, boils, risings, hemorrhoids, dropsy, stomach disorders, tumors, swellings, and cuts. All were said to be cured by elder leaves in the form of juice, decoctions, or poultices, while merely sleeping on a pillow of dried leaves relieved hay fever. Pliny, the ancient Roman, declared that drinking elder leaves in wine counteracted the bites of venomous snakes.

But mystic superstitions also sounded warnings. In Germany a leafy branch inside a house brought ghosts, in England, the Devil. In Scotland branches over doors and windows prevented evil spirits from entering and a branch buried with a corpse kept witches away.

The awesome power of elder is now diminished to minor but reliable uses. An infusion of leaves sprayed into a room will rid it of mosquitoes and flies; applied on plants, it frees them from aphids and caterpillars. And farmers today confidently maintain that elder leaves in bags of stored grain banish marauding mice and moles.

AMERICAN ELM

American Elm   *Ulmus americana*   (Elm Family)

The elms are dying by the millions, victims of the fatal Dutch-elm disease. Out in the green New England countryside, their gaunt, leafless skeletons stand against the sky, while along the once tree-shaded streets of old towns, large, level-cut stumps mark their passing.

This disease first broke out in the Netherlands, ravaging the elms that held the dykes. English elms, including those bordering the approach to Windsor Castle in London, fell victim next.

Full in the midst a spreading elm displayed
His aged arms and cast a mighty shade;
Each trembling leaf with some light visions teems
And leaves impregnated with airy dreams.
         —Virgil

In the United States the disease first appeared in Ohio after logs of English elm infested with swarms of elm bark beetles—the insects that carry the fungus from infected to healthy trees—were imported for veneer.

By the 1970s, millions of elms were killed in the eastern two-thirds of the country, and the epidemic continues to spread westward. Though no true cure has been found, Lignasan, a chemical retardant developed by DuPont, has been somewhat successful in slowing down its spread.

For centuries before this botanical tragedy occurred, the elm and its leaves were valued for its healing, nourishing, guiding, and warning properties. Dioscorides and Pliny

both believed that elm leaves helped to close and heal wounds, and with vinegar even relieved the sores of leprosy. Pliny declared that a poultice of pounded leaves reduced the swelling in feet. Fifteen centuries later, John Gerard, the English herbalist, echoed the ancients when he wrote, "The leaves of Elm glew and heale up green wounds," adding, "The decoction of Elm leaves healeth broken bones very speedily if they be bathed therewith."

❉

For English gardeners the leaves of the elm tree served as a planting guide.

The tree under which George Washington stood to officially take command of the Continental Army on July 3, 1775 was believed to be an elm.

When the leaves reached the size of a mouse's ear, it was time to plant the barley. This rhyme came from Warwickshire:

> *When Elm leaves are as big*
> *as a penny.*
> *You must plant kidney beans*
> *If you mean to have any.*

❉

But sometimes the life cycle of the leaves served as an ominous prediction. When elm leaves fall out of season, they foretell a plague on the cattle.

❉

In early America, especially in New England after a long winter, elm leaves bestowed an even more important bene-fit: a pleasant and quick source of nourishment. Of all the leaves the set-tlers ate, elm leaves were considered the best for relieving hunger.

❉

American Elm

...and the elms,
Fade into dimness apace,
Silent.

—Matthew Arnold,
Rugby Chapel

Blue Gum Eucalyptus

BLUE GUM EUCALYPTUS

Blue Gum Eucalyptus   *Eucalyptus globulus*   (Myrtle Family)

High-growing, handsome, and healing, the blue gum eucalyptus of the South Pacific is one of the world's great trees; its stature, beauty, and recognized utility have earned it this honor. Introduced into many mild parts of the world, this eucalyptus has now become a distinctive ornament in Spain, Morocco, Italy, and also warm regions of the United States. Its long, pendulous leaves hang like a dark curtain from slender branchlets. Among its many visual attractions is the exfoliating outer bark, which peels away in long strips to reveal a pale blue-gray trunk that gives the tree its the common name of blue gum.

This tall eucalyptus is not only beautiful, it is also economically important—the tree itself for erosion control and protective windbreaks; its dense lumber for fences, building, and furniture; and the bark for tanning and paper. The leaves, with their recognized therapeutic properties, further enhance its value.

In Australia, where it is sometimes called fever tree, eucalyptus played an

Wrap eucalyptus leaves in cheesecloth and let bathwater run over it to create a refreshing bath experience.

~ 129 ~

important role in folk medicine. Vapor from boiling leaves was used as an inhalant for diphtheria, and the smoke from burning leaves was believed to ease asthma. The leaves, rolled into cigarette-form, were smoked, and the smoke inhaled to clear the catarrhal discharges of bronchitis.

❧

While some of the other leaves once embraced by folk healers have been ultimately found to lack true curative power, eucalyptus leaves continue to this day to enjoy the blessing of scientific medicine. Appearing in the pharmacopoeias of several countries, eucalyptol, a derivative, is reliable for treating ulcers, wounds, sore throats, croup, and

To keep bugs out of your kitchen, soak cloths in eucalyptus oil and place them near problem areas.

spasmodic throat disorders.

❧

The leaves are also valuable for animals. The oil from the leaves is administered to horses for influenza, to dogs for distemper, and to all animals for parasitic skin infections. But for another animal, the Australian koala bear, these leaves are not only valuable, they are vital. The koala spends its placid life high in a eucalyptus tree, feeding exclusively on leaves of intermediate age (ranging from twelve to eighteen months old). Investigations have verified that younger leaves lack sufficient oil for good nourishment, while older ones contain enough prussic acid to kill a koala. Instinctively this small, pouch-bearing marsupial is able to detect fine differences that trained chemists can ascertain only with difficulty.

❧

COMMON FIG

Common Fig   *Ficus carica*   (Mulberry Family)

The common fig tree is one of our oldest plant companions. Ancient peoples were familiar with its sweet, seedy fruit, and in Mediterranean countries it was once known as food of the poor, as it was one of the main sources of nourishment for those with little money or property. Pliny, the Roman scholar, claimed in his writings that figs furnished much of the diet of slaves.

Originating in Asia Minor, this tree spread to India, then throughout the entire Mediterranean region. It now grows worldwide wherever winters are mild.

These fruitful trees are referred to in the Bible fifty-seven times, more than any other plant. The most famous allusion is found in Genesis 3:7. In relating the story of the fall of man and the expulsion of Adam and Eve from Eden, it says, "And the eyes of them both were opened, and they knew they were naked, and they sewed fig leaves together and made themselves aprons."

Since that famous biblical reference, fig leaves have been used as a covering, both sculpturally, as on statues of the male, and figuratively, as in the proverb, "The naked truth need no fig leaf."

Common Fig

They shall sit every man
under his vine, and
under his fig tree.

—Micah 4:4

But fig leaves not only covered, they
also cured—or so early healers believed.
Gerard, in his *Herbal*, praising them
extravagantly and at length, wrote,
"The leaves of the Figge tree do waste
and consume the King's Evill (scrofula)
or swelling kernels of the throat, and do
mollify, waste, and consume all other
tumors being finely pound and laid
thereon…The milky juice either of the
figges or leaves, is good against all
roughnesse of the skinne, lepries,
spreading sores, small pockes, measels,
pushes, wheales, freckles,
lentiles and scurvinesse
of the body and face,
being mixed with Barley
meale and applied it doth take away
warts and such like excrescence if it be
mingled with some fattie or greasie
thing." According to him, all these
medical wonders were achieved with
these handsome, green leaves. He then
ended with this homely bit of advice:
"Garlic with Figge leaves and Cumin is
laid on against the bitings of the mouse."

Gerard's medical counsel endured,
influencing herbalists for many years.
Later practitioners of folk medicine
modified his all-inclusive claims, merely
advising that a tea made of finely cut fig
leaves steeped in boiling water healed
sores, bruises, and inflamed throats.

When fishes flew and forests walked
And figs grew upon thorn,
Some moment when the moon was blood
Then surely I was born.

—G. K. Chesterton
Wild Knight and Other Poems

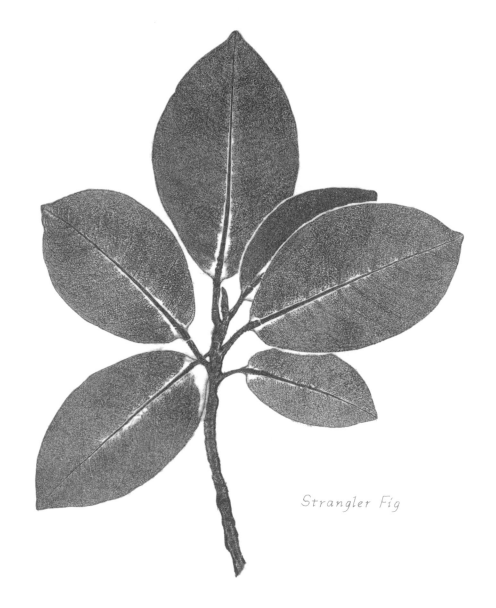

Strangler Fig

STRANGLER FIG

Strangler Fig   *Ficus aurea*   (Mulberry Family)

Though it is hard to believe, there is struggle and violence—even murder—in the peaceable kingdom of plants. One perpetrator of such botanical tragedy is the strangler fig of Florida. The beleaguered victim is a palm, usually the common and ubiquitous cabbage palmetto whose life is eventually sacrificed so that this aggressive fig tree may live.

To the casual observer, it appears that the roots of the fig are strangling the very life from the palm. Though these twisting, encircling roots certainly do the palm no good, in reality it is the lustrous green leaves of the fig that are the villain in this bizarre drama. This

mortal struggle has its beginnings when the minute seed of a fig passes unharmed through the digestive tract of a bird, a fruit-eating bat, or perhaps a squirrel. If the seed then falls into a moist, debris-filled pocket on the rough trunk of a palm, it germinates, and a young fig tree is born. As it develops, the fig tree sends down pliant roots,

which twine around the trunk of the host tree. The roots reach the earth and the branches of the fig grow upward, striving to hold their leaves ever higher toward the light. As the years pass, its roots become firmly established in the earth and the fig tree continues to grow and flourish, until finally its luxuriant leaves cut off all the life-giving sunlight from the palm, literally shading it to death. Gradually the trunk of the dead palm begins to decay, then completely rots away and disappears.

🌿

This predatory strangler fig is a member of the large and otherwise admirable Fig genus, a huge plant group containing more than eight hundred trees, shrubs, and woody vines, most of which grow in mild climates. Many are useful; some produce sweet, edible fruit; some furnish materials for fodder, for bark cloth, and also natural rubber. Others, because of their handsome evergreen leaves, are planted in parks and gardens for shade and ornament, while still others, like the large-leafed rubber tree and the glossy Benjamin fig, also grace conservatories and indoor gardens.

🌿

This particular fig tree, the Florida strangler fig, because of its interesting but wicked ways, is unique among North American trees.

FRINGE TREE

Fringe Tree   *Chionanthus virginicus*   (Olive Family)

The local differences in the common names of many plants reflect the individual fancy or personal experience of the namer. The many descriptive names of this tree vary from place to place and range from the sinister to the poetic.

❦

This tree has been called "poison ash"; it is in the same family as the ash trees, but no recorded evidence of its toxicity has been found. Next, there is "old man's beard," also "grandfather gray-beard," the narrow-petalled flowers obviously suggesting the hairy strands of a beard. This tree is sometimes called "flowering ash," "snow drop," or "snow flower," which is the precise English equivalent of its scientific name, *Chionanthus*, a lovely Greek word combining "snow" and "flower." However, "fringe tree" is the most common of its names and an understandable description of its hanging flowers.

❦

Dr. John Brickell, a visiting Irish physician, observed the native American fringe tree, and recorded it in the diary of his New World travels. "The leaves and flowers," he wrote, "are good in all inflammations and soreness of the eyes, ulcers in the mouth and throat, looseness of the gums, and to stop the fluxes." It is not known whether he made these claims from his own practical investigations, or whether they came by word of mouth from settlers in the area. It is, however, known that the fringe-tree leaves were also used in the folk medicine of the American South— as a tonic, a diuretic, and for intermittent fever.

🐝

The leaves of the fringe tree were once considered effective for "yaws," a serious skin disease resembling syphilis. This contagious illness, Frambesia, is caused by a microorganism, and is characterized by red lesions which can produce deformity if left untreated. Today, it is cured with penicillin.

🐝

The former country use of fringe-tree leaves may have medical validity. The leaves of other plants in the same family, notably privet and the olive tree, have been found to contain antibiotic substances.

An infusion of tea made from the bark of the fringe tree is thought to prevent gallstones.

Fringe Tree

GINGKO

Gingko   *Gingko biloba*   (Gingko Family)

Darwin had a prophetic name for the gingko tree; he called it a "living fossil." The gingko family was once a vast, dominant group of prehistoric trees that grew from Alaska to Greenland to England and reached the peak of their development during the Triassic and Jurassic eras, a time when dinosaurs still roamed the earth. The Ice Age exterminated these wild trees from the western hemisphere, all except for the *Gingko biloba*—the only surviving species, unchanged for over 200 million years. And until 1914, when one was found growing naturally in a corner of China's Chekiang province, it was known only as a tree of Asian temple gardens, believed saved from complete extinction by the care of Buddhist monks. Even today, the gingko is considered a sacred tree in their monastery gardens, a precious living link between the remote past and the modern world.

In America, the first recorded gingko—a tree brought from England in 1784 by William Hamilton—was planted in the Woodland Cemetery near Philadelphia. Today the gingko is often planted along city streets for its beauty, but is esteemed even more because its handsome leaves resist insects, drought, fungus, disease, and especially air pollution. One botanical writer declared, "It will grow even at the pavement's edge where buses breathe

Ginkgo

their unbreathable breath."

Not only are gingko leaves disease-resistant, but the Chinese and Japanese believe that they can also repel fire, an idea seemingly substantiated by one strange occurrence. A fire that destroyed much of Tokyo in 1923 spared an important temple that was surrounded by gingko trees. As an explanation, it was then theorized that the leaves of the gingko exude a repelling moisture when threatened by fire.

GINGKO PORRIDGE
(A Chinese recipe)

1 cup rice
2 cups water
About a dozen gingko nuts
Honey, to taste

Bring water to a boil. Stir in rice and gingko nuts. Lower heat to a simmer and cook for about 1 hour or until rice is cooked well. Blend well. Serve with honey, if desired, for sweetness.

In *Tales of a Shaman's Apprentice*, Dr. Mark Plotkin, a distinguished ethnobotanist and the vice president of plant conservation for Conservation International, reports important information on both ancient and modern medicinal uses for gingko leaves. For example, gingko extract has been used for more than five thousand years in China and Japan and has been considered effective against asthma and severe allergic inflammations. Today it is also widely used as a medicine in Europe; it is prescribed as a vasodilator (useful especially in treating the elderly for conditions caused by diminished blood flow to the brain) and is also believed helpful in treating asthma. Future applications are considered possible for kidney disorders, toxic shock, and the rejection of organ transplants.

GRAPE LEAF SKELETONIZER

Vitis species   *Harrisina americana*   (Vine Family)

Insect – Grape Leaf Skeletonizer

The grape leaf skeletonizer—a voracious insect with narrow, gauzy wings and a blue-black body—lays her eggs on the tender undersurfaces of grape leaves. In time, these clustered eggs hatch into yellow-and-black caterpillar larvae with long tufted, stinging hairs. Regimented into neat rows, these young larvae feed greedily on the under-surface of the leaves, leaving behind a network of intact leaf veins, of which, however, only the strong main veins remain. Thus the destruction of the leaf is complete.

❧

It is only natural that people deplore the ruin of their grape leaves, and that with noxious sprays they attempt to interrupt or end the destruc-tion, but for these growing insects, grape leaves are their very life.

❧

After sensitively observing a dam-aged leaf, American physician and gifted poet William Carlos Williams distilled a fine line of poetry: "And the eaten leaves are lace."

GRAPE VINE

Summer Grape *Vitis aestivalis* (Vine or Grape Family)

The native American summer grape belongs to the same distinguished family as the ancient biblical "vine," which according to that record was the first plant cultivated by humans. Grapes have been grown for so long by the human race—for seven to nine thousand years—that the original home of the vine cannot be determined with certainty. In this country, plant breeders have used the native fox grape—*Vitis labrusca*—a close relative of the summer grape, as one parent of hardy, cultivated American varieties, such as the concord, the catawba, and the chatauqua, and thus the long illustrious history of this simple, wild plant continues.

✻

The primary reason for our long love affair with the grape vine is, of course, the juicy fruit that is so delicious for food and wine. The leaves, however, have not been ignored. The renowned Greek physician Dioscorides succinctly declared, "To drink the juice of the leaves, doth help the dysenterical, the blood spitters and women that lust." He further advised that wild and cultivated leaves have the same virtues, recommending both for inflammations of the spleen, for snake bites, and as a poultice for headaches.

✻

Pliny, the Roman naturalist, concurred, adding that grape leaves benefit joint disease and staunch bleeding wounds.

The Native Americans used these leaves medicinally and, like the Greeks, bound their aching heads with cool grape leaves. In addition, they chewed the leaves to allay their thirst while on long marches.

The Greeks no longer heal themselves with grape leaves but enjoy them as an appetizer or main dish. *Dolma* are made by wrapping tender leaves around a mixture of rice combined with savory ingredients that may include lamb, beef, pine nuts, currants, onions, garlic, oregano, or thyme. The stuffed leaves are then cooked in broth and served hot or cold. When fresh leaves are unavailable, those preserved in jars take their place.

STUFFED GRAPE LEAVES

For fresh leaves: Select tender young leaves from top of vine, rinse under cold running water and place in a colander. Pour boiling water over leaves to soften; repeat if necessary.

For leaves in brine: Rinse well under running water and blanch in enough boiling water to cover to remove brine and soften leaves.

To stuff leaves: Prepare any one of several popular rice-stuffing varieties and fill the leaves using the following method:

Place filling near stem of leaf.

Fold base of leaf over filling.

Fold one side over bottom

Fold second side; roll up leaf.

And in a Winding sheet of
Vine-leaf wrapt, So bury me
by some sweet Garden-side.
  —Omar Khayam, Rubaiyat

Grape Vine

HARDHACK

Hardhack   *Spiraea tomentosa*   (Rose Family)

The aches and pains of early America were calmed, sometimes truly cured, with medicinal herbs. Even before the white man came, the Native Americans of the Northeast had discovered the healing uses of the small hardhack, knowledge perhaps later passed on to the new settlers.

The Shakers, a communal religious group that arrived from England in 1774, benefited medically and financially from this shared information. In time, they became America's most intrepid and productive herb gatherers, marketing their therapeutic botanicals widely and profitably, supporting their celibate societies with earnings from this activity. They were also the first in this country to package and sell plant seeds.

The women, called "sisters," made many day-long trips into the surrounding fields, swamps, and woods to gather literally thousands of pounds of herbs. Among many others, they collected and sold hardhack leaves, which were one of their most popular remedies. Like the Native Americans, they found these leaves useful for making an astringent tea to control diarrhea, dysentery, and other bowel complaints. The Shakers also prescribed hardhack as a diuretic, as well as for improving digestion, and for *cholera infantum*, commonly called "summer complaint."

❦

Though the Shakers as an active group have gradually died out, they left important chronicles of their daily lives and herbal gatherings in their "day books." These carefully kept records provide valuable insight into a specialized segment of American life.

❦

The Journal of Domestic Events and Transactions— 1843–1864 was a diary kept by the members of the New Lebanon, New York, group. In this record, in which they called hardhack "tea," and erroneously also by the name meadowsweet, a closely related European plant, the following entries appear: "June 27th: This morning a company of sisters start for Richmond swamp to gather tea. George L. starts with one horse wagon and James Gilbert takes the covered wagon. We start seven o'clock in the evening with a good load of meadowsweet tea.

"June 30th: Sisters go again after tea and have good luck.

"July 19th: Finishing and preparing and pressing tea.

"July 20th: Go to empty the press and clean up. Have 307 lbs. of tea."

❦

Hardhack

And every shepherd tells his tale
Under the hawthorn in the dale

—John Milton
L'Allegro

HAWTHORN

Hawthorn   *Crataegus Spp.*   (Rose Family)

Green grow the leaves on
the Hawthorn tree.
We jangle and we wrangle
And we never can agree.

These lines from an old English carol are prophetic. So appropriate is their message, they might almost have been written to describe the problems of the plant scientists who study the myriad species of the hawthorn now growing in America. The botanists specializing in this difficult plant group and the taxonomists who classify them do not always agree on the names, number, or validity of its many forms. Some say there are at least a thousand species, while others claim there are far fewer.

Though specialists argue and are baffled by the bewildering complexity of the hawthorns, wildlife suffers no such confusion. The edible red—sometimes yellow—applelike fruits that remain fresh on the branch for months after ripening are highly sought after by birds and small woodland animals. The densely twigged and thorny branches are a protective haven for the nests of many songbirds. Bees, too, seek out the springtime blossoms, making the hawthorn an important tree for honey making. And in England dense hawthorn hedges enclose horses and cattle in pasture and provide the animals with leaves to eat.

Because hundreds of species grow worldwide, hawthorn leaves have invaded the myths, magic, and folklore of many cultures. In ancient Athens, the leaves, a symbol of hope, were ritually chewed at funerals and purification rites, and girls on their wedding days wore them as crowns. The Romans concocted a potent tea of leaves as a charm against witches' spells, and leaves scattered in cradles protected delicate newborns. Early Christians believed a sprig of hawthorn delivered ships at sea from storms, and on shore, it rendered people safe from lightning. On May Day, the early Celts prudently decorated their

barns with its branches to ensure an abundant supply of summer milk.

❧

These fabled leaves also reputedly healed the ill. Pliny, a first-century Roman naturalist, declared that hawthorn leaves in wine relaxed the spasms of lockjaw, and even as late as the nineteenth century, England's *Family Receipt Book* still recommended a tea of hawthorn leaves combined with sage and balm as "an excellent sanative tea particularly wholesome to nervous people." Halfway across the world, the Kwakiutl Indians of Canada chewed hawthorn leaves into a poultice useful for reducing swelling; they also smoked the leaves as tobacco.

❧

And this tree of many virtues, beauteous in blossoms, bright with autumn fruit, and green with magical leaves, is now widely planted by landscapers.

In England, the hawthorn is known as the mayflower tree, in honor of the month during which it blooms. Symbolizing hope, it was the name the Pilgrims took for their famous ship, the Mayflower.

Hawthorn

The fair maiden who, the first of May,
Goes to the fields at the break of day
And washes in dew from the Hawthorn tree
Will ever after handsome be.

—Neltje Blanchan
Nature's Garden (1900)

AMERICAN HAZEL

American Hazel/Filbert *Corylus americana* (Birch Family)

The sharp-eyed country people who observed plants and gave them their common names were often amazingly accurate. Some early plant-watcher noticed the protective green covering encircling the developing nuts of this shrub and bestowed the name of "Haesle," an old Saxon word meaning a "cap." Later Anglicized, this became the name of our native American "hazel."

❋

Today, the preferred name for this shrub, and its delicious nuts, is filbert which harks back to an earlier time and is named for "St. Philibert," a Frankish abbot whose feast day, August 20th, falls during the nutting season.

❋

Not only is the hazel treasured for its delicious nuts but also because of its handsome green leaves which are cultivated in America as an attractive horticultural specimen. The irregular branches are also prized for making unique flower arrangements. However, though the leaves of our native hazel are admired for their beauty, they have not acquired any particular lore, legend, or special use in herbal medicine.

❋

On the contrary, the leaves of the very similar European hazel or filbert have earned themselves an interesting aura of superstitions for good omens and protective power.

❋

Medieval pilgrims venturing forth on

foot to distant, holy shrines, braving dangers day and night from cutthroats and thieves, kept themselves safe by binding hazel branches to their wayfarers' staves.

꧁

In England, small branches of these leaves gathered on Palm Sunday and kept alive indoors in water were said to protect the house from thunder and lightning. In Wales, fresh hazel leaves worn as a chaplet for the head brought general good luck; more specifically, they ensured the granting of wishes. This same leafy wreath worn at sea protected the vessel from shipwreck.

꧁

American Hazel

HEATHER

Heather *Calluna vulgaris* (Heath Family)

eather, a small, fine-twigged shrub, is a tough, sturdy dwarf. Because it rarely appears in North America, one botanist has termed it "a waif from Europe," where, as well as in Asia, it is truly at home. Enduring and tenacious, clinging to life under the most difficult conditions, heather sometimes grows only a few inches above the ground in barren wastelands where other plants can exist but barely, or not at all.

Every Scottish Highlander has a warm spot in his heart for this small, durable shrub with its feathery spikes of tiny, pink flowers. This affectionate association goes back centuries to a time when heather was a most use-ful plant, when its stems were used to make brushes, brooms, and bedding, and its stems and branches were cemented together with miry mud from peat bogs to make strong and long-lasting huts; in addition, the roofs were thatched with heather. Even today, farm sheds are made in this manner.

Serving in yet another way, minuscule heather leaves and young, tender tips were once the source of an ale. The modern way of making heather ale, as it is done today in the Scottish Lowlands, is described in *The Scot's Kitchen* by Marion McNeil. The recipe begins, "Crop the heather when it is in full bloom, enough to fill a large pot." Besides the leaves, flowers, and young stems of heather, the ingredients for

Heather

I never saw a Moor—
I never saw the Sea—
Yet know I how the Heather looks
And what a Billow be.

—*Emily Dickinson*

this brew include hops, yeast, syrup, ginger, and water; presumably, the heather adds a special flavor. The last line of the directions reads, "This makes a very refreshing and wholesome drink, as there is a good deal of spirit in heather."

Scottish animals have benefited from—even thrived on—this small native shrub. For the hardy, Highland sheep who graze on stony, upland pastures, heather's miniature, scale-like leaves and sinewy stems are an important source of fodder. Wild deer, as well, browse on this sparse but nourishing foliage.

While purple heather is common, white heather is quite rare and considered a symbol of good luck.

Eastern Hemlock

EASTERN HEMLOCK

Eastern Hemlock   *Tsuga canadensis*   (Pine Family)

The eastern hemlock, a tall, dark beauty of northern American woodlands, covers itself with short-needled foliage and small, pendant cones. When these northern forests were endless, and good timber and tan bark plentiful, these trees were spared, but when supplies of other economically valuable trees began to dwindle, the large virgin stands of stately hemlocks were doomed.

This forest tree with feathery branches is often seen as a handsome ornamental in parks and gardens. In areas where hemlock grows naturally, the young trees are sometimes planted, then continuously clipped and trimmed in order to create a high, thick, almost impenetrable evergreen hedge.

Immature hemlocks, unlike young spruces, firs, and balsams, are rarely ravaged for Christmas trees because their short needles dry up and fall off soon after they are cut down.

Their fresh branches have, however, had other, more pressing use, thanks to the resinous fragrance of their needles. The Native Americans of the Great Lakes region, the Ojibwas, Potawatamis, and the Menominees of Wisconsin all brewed a tea of these aromatic needles,

This is the forest primeval.
The murmuring pines and hemlocks…
Stand like Druids of old

—Henry Wadsworth Longfellow
Evangeline

drinking it as hot as could be tolerated to induce a copious perspiration effective for breaking up colds; for hot steam baths, they placed wet, green foliage over heated stones. And for tribal purification rites, as well as for therapeutic cleansing, they lashed their naked bodies while standing in water—even in winter—with green hemlock boughs.

🌿

Later the colonists adapted this knowledge to their own needs. A pillow of fresh hemlock needles, they believed, dispelled hay fever as long as the scent remained; for painful rheumatism in the loins, they sat on a bed of green hemlock boughs.

🌿

American lumbermen working in the cold, north woods, like the Native Americans, learned to concoct a strong, hot tea from the spicy needles. Other

Americans favored a similar tea made only of young hemlock tips steeped in boiling water, then sweetened with maple sugar. This brew, they claimed, refreshed and purified their system after the frigid northern winters.

🌿

Senecan lore tells of a hunter who challenged the spirit of winter, Hotho (He, the Cold One), claiming that nothing the spirit could do would cause the hunter to freeze. The hunter stayed awake all through the progressively colder night, but kept himself warm with a continual fire and by drinking a large kettleful of hemlock tea. At dawn, Hotho appeared to the hunter and admitted defeat, whereupon the earth began to grow warm and the ice and snow melted. The moral of this Senecan story is that humans can triumph over winter.

HENNA

Henna   *Lawsonia inerma*   (Loosestrife Family)

The use of henna for an orange-red dye is as ancient as the pyramids; the enduring stained nails of mummies exhumed from Egyptian tombs proclaim its antiquity.

❦

In the sixth century, the prophet Mohammed dyed his beard with henna, a fashion then adopted by the Muslim caliphs, the regional leaders. In North Africa today, Arabs still dye hair, nails, palms of hands, and soles of feet with henna, a custom they claim is cooling and beautiful, and even the manes and tails of their Arabian horses are colored with this red-brown dye.

❦

It is the leaves of this sweet, flowering shrub native to North Africa, Asia, and Australia that produce this long-lasting reddish color. In Morocco dried henna leaves for use as a dye are displayed in bins in labyrinthine markets called *souks*. At home, leaves and small twigs are pounded fine and mixed with water to create a paste that is applied to the hair and left on overnight. To vary the shade, this preparation is sometimes combined with catechu, an extract from wood or lucerne leaves, a type of alfalfa. For a deep-black shade that lasts for three to four weeks, the hair is first dyed with henna, then with indigo, another colorant extracted from leaves.

❋

In nineteenth-century Europe henna was a popular shampoo, and today in America dried henna leaves that can be used to add reddish highlights to the hair are sold at some natural food shops and herbal pharmacies. The process is simple and harmless: Soak two tablespoons of dried leaves in one cup of warm water overnight. The next morning strain the mixture, retaining the liquid and discarding the leaves, and add one tablespoon of alcohol to the liquid. Wash and towel dry the hair, then use the tinted liquid as a finishing rinse.

Chieftain Iffucan of Azcan in caftan
Of tan henna hackles, halt!

—Wallace Stevens,
Bantam in the Pine Woods

❋

Though generally unknown and unused today, henna as a medicinal is as ancient as the dye. In the first century, it was familiar to Dioscorides, who wrote, "The leaves have a binding power wherefore being chewed they help the ulcers of the mouth, and being applied as a cataplasme [poultice], they cure all other hotte inflammations and carbunkles."

❋

Folk healers in the Near East also prescribed henna, both internally and externally, for jaundice, liver trouble, and afflictions of the skin, even leprosy. One bizarre ancient reference to this medicine claimed that henna leaves pounded fine and applied to the navel during a fever drew all evil impurities from the body.

❋

Henna

HICKORY LEAF

Hickory Tree   *Carya spp.*   (Hickory Family)
Insect – Leaf-cutter Bee   *Megachile latimanus*

eatly cut and oddly scalloped, this incised hickory leaf bears mute witness to the importance of leaves to insects—in this instance, to the leaf-cutter bee. Its Greek scientific name, *Megachile latimanus* (*mega*, meaning strong or great; *cheilos*, meaning lip), translates to strong-lipped bee, and it is with its powerful lip that this bee bites out round or oval pieces from the margins of leaves, frequently rose leaves. Rolling up these cut leaf sections, one by one, between its legs, the bee flies to certain selected sites where it has already fashioned thimble-shaped brood cells, either by burrowing into the earth or rock crevices or, alternatively, into the hollow stems of plants. After the bee has lined the cell walls with leaves, it places inside a nourishing ball of pollen, a drop of nectar, and an egg. Finally, with a disk cleverly cut a little larger than the diameter of the cell to ensure a snug fit, it seals the precious life inside.

❧

The leaf-cutter bee is an important pollinator of grain, alfalfa, and other legumes. In the West, on large alfalfa-producing farms, growers provide artificial nesting sites for these indispensable insects.

❧

During the war of 1812, Andrew Jackson led a troop of Tennessee backwoodsmen and frontiersmen. He so impressed them with his courage and stamina that they dubbed him Old Hickory. During his 1828 election campaign, voters would show their support by erecting hickory posts on their property.

Leaf Cutter Bee

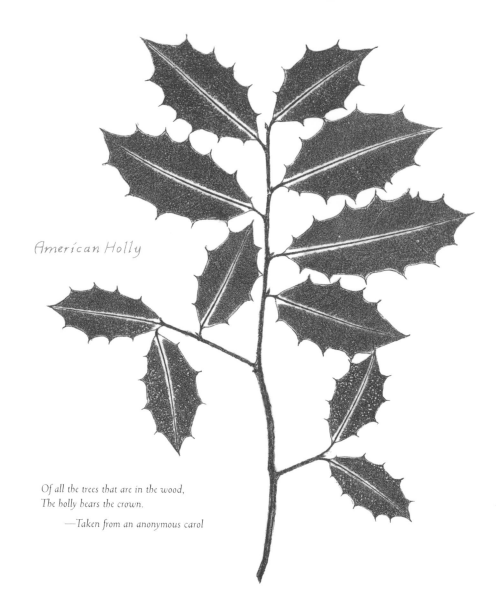

American Holly

Of all the trees that are in the wood,
The holly bears the crown.

—Taken from an anonymous carol

AMERICAN HOLLY

American Holly   *Ilex opaca*   (Holly Family)

To the ancients, holly was a holy tree, lucky and potently protective. Its spiny, leathery leaves were thought to have the mysterious power to avert the evils of witchcraft, the perils of lightning, spells, and malignant demons. These early beliefs are the distant roots of the holiday custom of adorning our homes with holly.

Reflecting these time-honored ideas, the words of an old English carol urged people to "Deck the halls with boughs of holly." Since holly was considered a magic plant in England, this decorating with it was guided by certain mystic rules. For example, holly could not be brought into the house before Christmas, and it had to be taken down on Twelfth Night. It was said that one misfortune would befall for each leaf left past that time.

In medieval England, still other superstitions surrounded these leaves. For example, an unmarried woman was urgently advised to tie a sprig of holly to the bedpost to avoid being turned into a witch. And to see in a dream her future mate, a girl was advised to go outside, pick nine holly leaves, tie them with nine knots in a three-cornered handkerchief, then lay them on her pillow before going to sleep, all without uttering a word before dawn.

Here in America, we have inherited

some of those old customs, but most of the quaint, mystical ideas have been diluted or lost through distance and time. We do, however, deck our homes and halls with holly and, in fact, we decorate so abundantly that to supply the popular demand, our eastern woodlands are being depleted of this festive adornment. To conserve the holly, many states have now proclaimed it a protected plant. To further save the wild trees, a new horticultural industry has emerged— commercial holly farming. One farm in southern New Jersey goes by the amusing name of Cholly's Holly Farm.

Unaware of Europe's holly traditions, Native Americans developed their own uses for these prickly leaves. They brewed a healing tea for measles, and from the ashes of the leaves they concocted another tea for whooping cough. To ease the pain of broken bones and dislocations, they applied hot fomentations of leaves and bark.

Euell Gibbons, a well-known American naturalist and author, perhaps influenced by early Native American medicine, advocated the therapeutic use of holly-leaf tea to induce perspiration and to reduce the fever accompanying pleurisy.

In the American language of flowers, holly symbolizes foresight.

INDIGO

Indigo   *Indigofera dosua*   (Pea Family)

Forty centuries ago there were three celebrated dyes for making fabric—and life—more colorful: purple, scarlet, and blue. The purple dye, called Tyrian purple, came from the glands of murexes (a kind of mollusk). The scarlet dye was created from the bodies of the kermes insect. And that famous ancient blue dye was derived from the leaves and stems of indigo, a modest shrub with a history stretching back over four thousand years.

Ancient India was the first home of the indigo plant, and also the place where the name "indigo" originated. Indians were the first to raise indigo and to understand the method for extracting color from its small leaves. From India, traders brought the plant and its technology to the Mediterranean region and from there it spread to the rest of the world. The ancient Egyptians, Greeks, and Romans grew and used indigo, calling it the "king of dye-stuffs." The early people of Nigeria also knew it, processing it in earthen pits before sending it into the interior of Africa.

Seventeenth-century trading ships brought indigo to America, where it was established in the warm, southern colonies from Georgia through the Carolinas and into Virginia. There, the leaves became a dye by the same ancient method employed by

Indigo

earlier civilizations, a complicated, time-consuming, and malodorous process and made possible and profitable by the abundant slave labor of the plantations.

❦

Exported to England, this American dyestuff was of such excellent quality and so enthusiastically received that it fetched premium prices. This trade with England was short-lived, however, brought to an abrupt close by the American Revolution. Later, to protect their own industries, other countries also refused to accept American indigo or levied unprofitably high import duties. By the early 1800s, indigo was no longer an American export crop.

❦

In 1856, William Perkin, an English chemist, made a stunning breakthrough discovery that sounded the death knell for this and other botanical dyes. In that year, he developed a method for creating a purplish-blue dye from coal-tar products. Then in 1883, German chemist Adolf von Beyer perfected a method for the laboratory synthesis of this dye, which made it commercially viable.

❦

Today only craftspeople specializing in natural materials use indigo leaves to create that unique color known as indigo blue. Here and there, wild specimens, descendants of the earlier, planted indigo, still grow in our southern states.

Now four great indigo spindles,
her harvest, her doom,
rage blue in her nightly sleeps, only hers;
day after day at four she stirs;
with dawn's first ray she leaps at the loom;
fingers of parchment, shuttle of rust,
Old mates, they know the way,
but always the thrust, the throb is new,
once more a begetting, once more a breed of blue.
—Aaron Kramer
"Indigo" from Indigo and Other Poems

English Ivy

Oh roses for the flush of youth,
And laurel for the perfect prime;
But pluck an ivy branch for me
Grown old before my time.
            —Song (1862)
    by Christina Georgina Rossetti

ENGLISH IVY

English Ivy   *Hedera helix*   (Aralia or Ginseng Family)

Evergreen ivy, an ancient companion of man, famous in magic, myth, and medicine, is a plant the Greeks once knew and honored by weaving fables around its leaves. They created a fanciful story to explain the disparity between two types of ivy leaves: one, a lobed leaf of infinite variety and another with a simple unlobed heart shape.

❧

The tale told of a young male dancer and drinking companion of Dionysus, the god of wine, who while dancing with wild abandon to please the god fell dead of exhaustion. In tender memory of his beloved friend, Dionysus then commanded the ivy henceforth to bear heart-shaped leaves. The illustra-tion here and on the following page shows both leaf forms.

❧

In England it was once believed that if ivy refused to grow on a grave it meant the soul was unhappy in its other world. If it flourished on a young girl's grave, it meant she died of unrequited love. For predicting the outcome of illness and other matters of health, ivy leaves were infallible. Pressing a leaf against her heart, a girl would hopefully repeat:

Ivy, Ivy I love you
In my bosom I put you
The first young man who
  speaks to me,
My future husband he shall be.

❧

Hippocrates, the pre-Christian "father of medicine," included magical ivy in his herbal remedies, and, influenced by him, later herbalists considered ivy a curative plant. Pliny, the Roman naturalist, believed it was a diuretic, relieved headaches, and benefited the brain. Later, two English botanic healers, Gerard and Culpeper, both claimed that ivy cured many illnesses, both minor and severe.

*

The incredible list of specific disorders for which ivy has been prescribed reveals its long-standing, exalted reputation: bad spleens, baldness, bloody flux, bunions, catarrh, colds, corns, dropsy, gallstones, intoxication, jaundice, plague, poisoning, rheumatism, skin infections, sore eyes, swollen glands, ulcers, worms, wounds—and more.

*

Out of this questionable catalog of ills, some reputable facts have emerged. It is now scientifically established that all parts of the ivy plant are poisonous if ingested, the toxic principle being hederin, a dangerous compound that can cause dermatitis, illness—even death. But ivy also has good uses, and is now reliably known to be antibiotic, effective against fungi and certain bacteria.

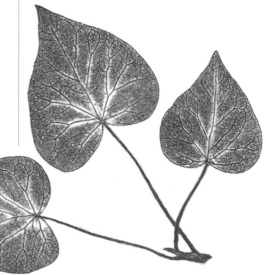

COMMON JUNIPER

Common Juniper   *Juniperus communis*   (Cypress Family)

The common juniper, a sprawling shrub with needled leaves, has one most uncommon, even unique, distinction. Some botanists claim that this is the only woody plant that is truly at home on three continents—Europe, Asia, and North America. With such widespread growth, it is no surprise that its reputed virtues have been many.

⁂

One frequently recorded concern of old herbal medicine was finding antidotes against poisons. And among the many benefits attributed to juniper leaves is protection against vipers. The ancient Greek physician Dioscorides and the English herbalists Gerard and Culpeper all praised the special power of juniper. John Gerard claimed that the smoke of the wood and leaves drove vipers away, while Dioscorides and Culpeper recommended applying a poultice of the leaves, or drinking their juice in wine, to counteract a viper's poisonous bite.

⁂

Of all the herbal healers who prescribed the benefits of juniper, none was more uncritically convinced than Culpeper. Beyond claims of protection against vipers, he extravagantly asserted that the

During World War II, French nurses would burn juniper in hospital rooms, believing the smoke prevented bubonic plague and leprosy.

Common Juniper

juniper "is scarce to be paralleled for its virtues." He then proceeded to list seventeen other ills benefited by this shrub, most of them serious, including consumption and falling sickness (epilepsy). He also wrote that juniper was effective "for strengthening the brain."

❧

The Native Americans brewed teas of juniper needles for relieving earaches, constipation, colic, and rheumatism. They boiled and ate the tender-tipped leaves for an upset stomach, or applied them as a poultice to reduce the inflammation of wounds. To fumigate the delivery area after childbirth, they used the cleansing smoke of burning leaves.

❧

Country healers in the Appalachian mountains prescribed the oil extracted

Fresh or dried juniper berries are an excellent addition to marinades for meat or game.

The distinct flavor of gin is attributed to the juniper berry.

from juniper needles for dropsy, liver complaints, and rheumatism. Even today the oil is rubbed on aching backs and the steam from the boiling leaves is still inhaled for bronchitis.

❧

In other countries the mere fragrance of juniper leaves made life more pleasant. In India they were burned as incense, and in Spain spicy chorizo sausages were seasoned with smoke from burning green branches; the resinous leaves themselves flavored home-brewed beer in Norway and Finland. A fanciful old Italian superstition claims that a juniper bush kept by the door of a house would prevent a witch from entering because before she could pass it, she would have to correctly count its number of needles.

KHAT

Khat   *Catha edulis*   (Staff-Tree Family)

Khat is a modest evergreen shrub whose entrancing leaves have changed the life of one small Asian country. This shrub, though truly native to East Africa, is now widely planted in Yemen, where it is at once the source of a pleasant social activity, a cash crop for farmers, and an actively contested national issue.

🌿

In northern Yemen, one of the world's poorest areas, coffee was once the most important crop and a prime source of income for farmers. Coffee trees, however, require much tiring labor, including frequent pruning and the tedious work of handpicking the ripe berries.

🌿

Khat, on the other hand, thrives in poor soil, requires little water, and is an easy, lucrative crop that can be gathered frequently, the green harvest consisting of leafy branches cut and tied into bundles. Even though khat is expensive, it finds a ready market among the people because of Yemen's new prosperity.

🌿

Its present relative affluence originated in the Western world's thirst for Arab oil. Though Yemen has no oil of its own, foreign money flows into that country because one third of its men emigrate periodically to Saudi Arabia to work in the oil fields, bringing their earnings home with them.

🌿

Though its use has been known since antiquity, the chewing of khat has now become almost an obsession, enjoyed by men as a group recreation. Resting on cushions while conversing quietly, the men pinch off the leaves, then chew and suck them for hours. They claim that khat is harmless when used with restraint and produces only a gentle euphoria, a stimulation equal only to the effect of several cups of coffee. Reportedly, the adverse effects are mild sleeplessness and a slight loss of appetite. Those opposing this practice—visiting foreigners and Yemeni officials—claim that the use of khat is a waste of people's time and, worse, a waste of a family's income.

Those who decry this custom know that the only way to root it out is to provide other, more attractive forms of recreation, and an easier, more lucrative cash crop for Yemen's farmers. Nothing has emerged so far to fill these needs.

Khat

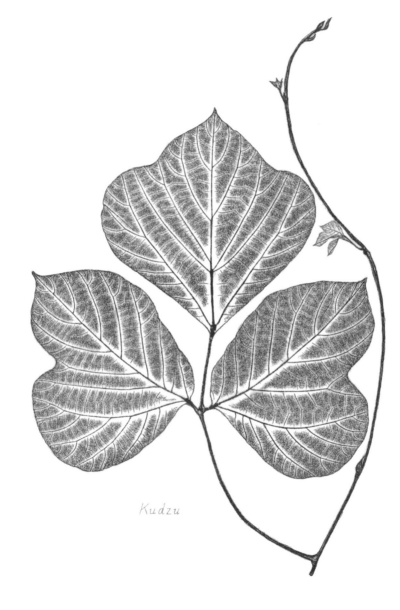

Kudzu

KUDZU

Kudzu   *Pueraria lobata*   (Pea or Pulse Family)

The irrepressible kudzu vine, which flourishes in southern states, is the subject of an ongoing controversy. Because it invades established croplands with incredible speed, some farmers advocate its total eradication, while others contend that instead, it should be put to innovative use. To that end, it is now the subject of serious research.

❧

Because of its prodigious rate of growth, kudzu, first introduced into the United States from its native Japan in 1876, has been facetiously called the "mile-a-minute vine," and "the only plant whose growth can be measured in miles per hour." When first introduced into America, kudzu was envisioned as a means of erosion control, a holding crop hailed as "the miracle vine," and "the savior of the South." One southerner praised it by saying, "Why, the whole state of Georgia would have washed down into the Atlantic Ocean if kudzu hadn't reached out, grabbed all that dirt, and held it back."

❧

The South is gradually becoming disenchanted with kudzu, first calling it "a nuisance," then "a scourge." One botanic writer even termed it "a vegetal form of cancer." A newspaper headline proclaimed, "The South is fighting another war, and losing once again."

❧

But in Japan, and to some extent in the United States, new uses are now being found for kudzu. High in nitro-gen, phosphoric acid, and potassium, cover crops of kudzu plowed into the earth become an enriching green manure. Today farmers are also using it as a nourishing forage plant for fattening livestock, including cattle, hogs, and poultry. And at Tennessee's Vanderbilt University, plant chemists are studying the possibility of turning the vines and leaves into fuel, and using the root as yeast.

❧

The inventive Japanese are converting

The fastest growing of all woody vines outside the warmer climates of North America, the kudzu vine may produce shoots 60 feet long in a single season. It climbs by twining but does so in a rather lazy manner; the shoots wind around their supports only a few times where vines like bittersweet would twine many times. The flowers and fruits of the kudzu vine are not ornamentally effective as they are mostly covered by the large leaves.

An old Chinese herbal cure for a hangover prescribes a tea made from the root and flowers of the kudzu.

the tender leaves of kudzu into human nourishment. Young leaves are steamed, boiled, or sautéed, and served with piquant sauces. Dried leaves are being made, with other ingredients, into breakfast cereal, and powdered kudzu is being added to noodles. As a food sup-plement, finely ground leaves are made into tablets rich in vitamins A and C, while green chlorophyll from the leaves, mixed with enzymes, fortifies health foods and natural medicines.

❧

Chinese doctors are also seriously experimenting with a substance extract-ed from kudzu leaves and stems for the control of high blood pressure and the relief of angina and migraines. The final verdict on the controversial kudzu vine is not yet in.

MOUNTAIN LAUREL

Mountain Laurel   *Kalmia latifolia*   (Heath Family)

Mountain laurel, a blossoming profusion of pink and white, is the glory of an Appalachian spring, the season when thousands of nature lovers make annual pilgrimages to see it in bloom. The shrubs bearing these clustered flowers are handsome whether growing wild in the mountains or planted in home shrubbery borders; their glossy, dark leaves are evergreen, elegant—and lethal when ingested.

❀

Domestic animals in fields bordered by laurel sometimes feed on this toxic foliage, especially during the winter if food is scarce. Sheep, especially the incautious young, have been victims. Calves, too, have been poisoned, but they were sometimes restored to life— at least it is claimed—by the legendary country remedy of gunpowder. According to a modern veterinarian and pharmacist, the saving ingredient in gunpowder may have been charcoal, which would have absorbed the poison of the leaves, allowing it to pass off harmlessly with body waste.

❀

Even zoo animals have died from laurel poisoning. Mountain laurel is sometimes planted in the parks surrounding city zoos. Visitors, unaware of the plant's extreme toxicity and in spite of posted warnings against feeding, have broken off leafy branches from the bushes and fed them to the animals.

❀

*Laurel is green for a season, and love is
sweet for a day;
But love grows bitter with treason,
and laurel outlives not May.*

—*Algernon Charles Swinburne*
Hymn to Proserpine

Reputedly only certain animals are adversely affected by laurel, suffering dizziness, abdominal pain, paralysis, or death; goats, deer, and birds seem to remain unharmed. Humans, however, are not immune. In fact, the Delaware Indians of the East drank a brew made with as little as two ounces of laurel leaves when they wanted to commit suicide.

❧

These leaves, though toxic, were once also considered effective in herbal medicines. An ointment made from leaves stewed in lard was a country remedy for the "itch" and other skin disorders, and salve that included the juice of the leaves, locally applied, eased rheumatism. A decoction of leaves banished fevers and jaundice, was a cardiac sedative, and stopped diarrhea and hemorrhaging. However, because of the hazardous nature of this remedy, it always needed to be administered with the greatest care.

❧

The American mountain laurel must not be confused with the true laurel (*Laurus nobilis*), a Mediterranean tree sometimes called the sweet bay tree, whose leaves are used in cooking. This error has been made in at least one cookbook and could lead to dangerous results.

Ah Nature! the very look of the woods is heroical and stimulating. This afternoon in a very thick grove where Henry Thoreau showed me the bush of mountain laurel, the first I have seen in Concord, the stems of pine and hemlock and oak almost gleamed like steel upon the excited eye.

—*Ralph Waldo Emerson,*
November 20, 1840, Journals

Mountain Laurel

LEMON VERBENA

Lemon Verbena   *Aloysia triphylla*   (Vervain Family)

emon verbena, an aromatic shrub that grows wild in South America, has fragrantly invaded gardens in warm climates all over the world. Its universal popularity lies not in impressive appearance or great beauty of flower, but rather in the lemon-sweetness of the tender leaves.

❋

Wherever it grows, its perfume is so compelling that people passing can rarely resist plucking a leaf. One frustrated gardener declared that he would never again have it in his garden because it was constantly being defoliated, carried away leaf by sweet-smelling leaf.

❋

Because the dried leaves of this verbena retain their lemony scent for a long time—even years—they are a frequent choice for sachets that scent closets and drawers as well as for bowls of potpourri. The chemical room deodorizers and fresheners available today are efficient but lack the gentle, enduring charm of natural plant fragrances.

❋

The oil extracted from the leaves of lemon verbena is also used in commercial perfumes, face creams, and other cosmetics.

❋

The importance of lemon verbena leaves in medicine has never equaled the importance of their bouquet. However, they have been the source of decoctions taken as sedatives and for diminishing indigestion.

❋

In southern Italy, use of lemon
verbena as a country medicinal is
more unusual. It is said that women
desiring children should always
drink a tea
brewed from these
leaves, though its
effectiveness is not sci-
entifically documented.

❋

Brazilians simply enjoy their
lemon verbena tea, which they
call *capitao do matto*, because they
like the way it tastes.

❋

Add lemon verbena leaves to
fresh fruit salads, fruit drinks,
and mint teas for flavor.

Lemon Verbena

American Linden

AMERICAN LINDEN

American Linden *Tilia americana* (Linden Family)

The American linden, also called basswood, is beautiful, useful, and in every way an admirable tree. Because of its attractive appearance, its fine stature and its branches thickly clad with handsome bright green leaves, the linden makes an excellent shade or street tree.

During the summer the pervasive fragrance of its creamy-white flowers announces its presence, even from hundreds of feet away. Bees come to this tree from far and wide and, forsaking all others, surround it in great, humming swarms. The honey they distill from the nectar of the blossoms is white, highly flavored, and much sought by connoisseurs.

The wood of this tree, though weak, is lightweight and, when dry, odorless and tasteless, making it ideal for food containers and for many other uses as well, including small woodenware, crates, a core for veneers, yardsticks, and, increasingly, paper pulp.

But the true glory of this splendid tree is its crown of large, asymmetrical, heart-shaped leaves, which are beautiful, healing, and nourishing. In herbal country medicine, infusions of the leaves and flowers were once prescribed as a soothing balm for colds, coughs, and headaches and for alleviating indigestion and eliminating catarrh. Taken hot, this tea induced sweating; warm baths scented with leaves and flowers promoted restful sleep.

✻

These leaves, fresh and green, nourished cattle in early America. When lindens, and in fact when all trees were plentiful, farmers wastefully felled them so their animals could browse on the foliage more easily. Dried and stored like hay, the leaves also provided winter fodder.

✻

Nourishing animals on linden leaves is an ancient tradition. Three centuries before Christ, Theophrastus, the Greek "father of botany," author of the world's oldest botanical treatise—*Enquiry Into Plants*—declared, "The leaves of linden

To relieve severe cramps or acid indigestion, steep one teaspoon of linden leaves and flowers in one cup of boiling water for two to seven minutes depending on strength desired.

are very sweet, and be a food for most kinds of cattell."

✻

The leaves of the European linden also inspired magical beliefs. In Scythia, an ancient country north of the Black Sea, local soothsayers twined linden leaves around their fingers while uttering prophecies, claiming that the trees spoke to them through their leaves. Later, in old Germany, perhaps also relying on the wisdom mysteriously expressed by leaves, magistrates considered the linden a tree of judgment and sat beneath its whispering greenery when passing sentences.

Red Mangrove

RED MANGROVE

Red Mangrove   *Rhizophora mangle*   (Mangrove Family)

According to the author John Steinbeck, "No one likes the mangroves." More recently, however, one enlightened conservationist, with valid reason, called it "the sacred tree of Florida," an opinion corroborated by studies at the University of Florida.

Visitors to Florida can't help wondering about these strange trees that seem to stand on stilts in the salty mud of the shore. Very few trees can flourish under the saline conditions in which mangroves thrive, and it is precisely their salt tolerance, as well as their queer, spidery legs, that make them valuable. Their arched prop roots catch silt and debris, eventually form land, and thus hold and extend the fragile shoreline.

The mangrove propagates and roots in an unusual way. After its yellow blossoms fall, brown fruits form; the seed within each fruit begins to germinate and, while still attached to the tree, develops into a twelve-inch seedling. If on dropping from the tree the seedling falls on land, the plant roots immediately, but if it falls into the water, it drifts with the current, even for months, until it touches earth where it can grow. Because of the seedling's unusually tenacious hold on life, it can remain alive during long sea voyages; from Florida it reaches distant destinations that include California,

Ecuador, Brazil, and even West Africa.

*

The power of the mangrove leaf is awesome; it is, of all the leaves presented in this book, perhaps the most valuable and exceedingly uncommon, the green starting point of an amazing, multi-leveled food chain. More than three tons of leaves are shed annually by a single acre of trees, a large portion of which fall into water. In Florida, marine life from the tiniest shrimp to the mightiest game fish depend on this prodigious leaf fall.

*

First fungi and microbes initiate the breakdown of the leaves by feeding on their carbohydrates. Later other minute creatures—protozoa and bacteria—attack, further decomposing the leaves. The resulting slimy, brown film attracts small, hungry organisms, nematodes and other marine worms, and tiny crustaceans that continually consume and break down the leaves and other attackers into protein-rich particles. Small fish feed on these worms and crustaceans, only to be consumed in their turn by larger fish.

*

Game fish, the commercially important mullet, and edible shrimp all depend on the mangrove for food and for protection among its roots. Initiated by leaves, this long, complex food chain, with its interconnecting links of birth, growth, death, and rebirth, ultimately benefits humans nutritionally, economically, and recreationally.

*

For the all-life-supporting power of its leaves, the mangrove must, indeed, be called sacred.

*

JAPANESE MAPLE

Japanese Maple *Acer palmatum* (Maple Family)

Poets everywhere have celebrated leaves, but of all the world's people, none more than those of Asia have expressed so often or so well their poetic kinship with them. Their special affection for maple leaves is legendary.

In the calendar of China, maple leaves symbolize October, while to the Japanese, these autumn leaves are akin to flowers as decorative elements. Each year in China and Japan, the seasonal color change of the maples attracts millions of viewers to public gardens and parks and to the grounds surrounding temples and shrines.

Among those entranced by maple leaves was Tu Mu, a Chinese poet of the ninth century who recorded in the poem "Roaming in a Mountain" his own sensitive appreciation of these colorful autumn leaves.

I halt my carriage and sit awhile,
To admire the maples in the eventide.
How the frost has dyed their leaves
To a deeper crimson than the
flowers of March.

The Japanese often express their closeness to nature in poems called haiku. Kenneth Yasuda, a Japanese-American poet, aptly defines the haiku as "a one-breath poem in three lines, a single flower of beauty whose petals are seventeen syllables, all told."

~ 193 ~

Envied by us all
The leaves of maple turn so
Beautiful, then fall
       —Shiko

The small maple, whose leaves have inspired these lines, is a conspicuously beautiful tree that came originally from Japan and which, since 1820, has been cultivated in America. This Japanese maple, dark red in summer, turning to fiery scarlet in fall, is perhaps the most elegant and graceful of the many Asian plants ornamenting American gardens today.

Japanese Maple

RED MAPLE

Red Maple   *Acer rubrum*   (Maple Family)

The maple leaf our emblem dear
The maple leaf forever,
God save our Queen, and heaven bless
The maple leaf forever.

❧

The Canadians sing this patriotic anthem to honor their country and queen. Because Canada abounds in maple trees, the maple leaf is the country's symbol and appears in red against the white portion of the Canadian flag. This emblematic symbol, though not an exact representation of any one species, is a composite leaf of two of the most common maples in Canada: the sugar maple and the red maple. Together, the two represent the fundamental maple-leaf shape.

❧

The common red maple earns its name by displaying a touch of red throughout the year. In winter, thin dark-red twigs bear blood-red buds, and in the spring the tree puts forth small crimson blossoms on its cool gray branches. Following these early flowers, the seeds—twin-winged samaras—radiate the same glowing shade of red. Even the green leaves of high summer possess red-tinted stems. And when the warm season ends, the red maple's flaming leaves herald the advent of autumn.

❧

According to botanists, the sugar trapped in the red maple's dying leaves is responsible for the fiery fall color. Describing this phenomenon, the American poet Robert Lowell wrote, "The maple swamps glow like a sunset at sea."

Red maple leaves, so spectacularly beautiful in autumn, have less than sensational practical uses. In early folk medicine, teas and decoctions brewed from the leaves were considered therapeutic for strengthening the liver, or, as one nature healer proclaimed, were good for, "easing the pains in the sides proceeding from liver and spleen."

The beneficial virtues of red maple leaves have been few; still worse, the leaves have, at times, been proven harmful. When eaten in quantity as forage, they can be toxic to animals. In his book *Poisonous Plants of the U.S. and Canada*, noted American plant toxicologist Dr. John Kingsbury cites the death of cattle and horses after eating red maple leaves.

Red Maple

EUROPEAN MISTLETOE

European Mistletoe   *Viscum album*   (Mistletoe Family)

To ancient man the evergreen mistletoe—living and thriving without thrusting roots into the earth—was a magical and mysterious plant. Today we understand its partly parasitical manner of existing on the life of its host tree, but to the pagan Druids of Britain it was an object of religious veneration.

In pre-Christian Britain, the Druids held solemn forest ceremonies in which the ritual cutting of the mistletoe with a golden sickle was accompanied by the sacrifice of two milk-white bulls.

This legendary plant, though frequently found on a variety of trees, only rarely grew on oak, but when it did, the Druids held that oak sacred, and the mistletoe growing on it a plant of supernatural medicinal power. Small, leafy pieces of this potent greenery distributed to the faithful were holy relics, capable of neutralizing poisons and warding off evil spirits.

Also, as a symbol of peace, it temporarily suppressed old hatreds. Enemies meeting in the forest beneath these holy leaves would kiss, exchange friendly greetings, and refrain from fighting for that day. This, some say, is possibly the distant origin of our holiday custom of

European Mistletoe

kissing under the mistletoe.

✿

Though diluted by time, remnants of old religious beliefs later emerged as folk superstitions. A mistletoe garland around the neck banished witches; a leafy branch hung by a door bespoke a welcome; leaves on the doorstep protected those within from nightmares; hung indoors, leaves repelled all evil, even lightning.

✿

Because mistletoe was once the principle symbol of Druidic paganism, Christian bishops in Britain forbade its use in holiday church decorations. The single exception to this prohibition was the York Cathedral, where each year a large offering of mistletoe was laid on the altar. There, called by its former name, all heal, it was the spiritual symbol of Christ, the "Divine Healer of Nations."

✿

Old medicine once prescribed mistletoe as a cure for nervous disorders, St. Vitus Dance, chorea, epilepsy, and "fits and fainting." European mistletoe is scientifically known to lower blood pressure, and for this it is still included in the French and Spanish pharmacopoeias, though it is also known to be potentially damaging to the heart.

✿

One final small but possibly significant note: modern medical research has discovered that the juice of these celebrated leaves inhibits tumors in mice.

Another possible origin for kissing under the mistletoe may have come from Norse mythology which tells of Balder, the god of peace who is killed by an arrow made of mistletoe. After bringing him back to life, his parents, the gods Odin and Frigga, give a mistletoe plant to the goddess of love, decreeing that whosoever passed under it should receive a kiss.

WHITE MULBERRY

White Mulberry   *Morus alba*   (Mulberry Family)

The leaves of the white mulberry tree have influenced history more than any others—except perhaps tea leaves. This unusual mulberry tree, which bears leaves essential for making silk, originally came from China; it now grows in many other parts of the world as well, including Asia Minor, Europe, and North America.

❧

For producing precious silk, there are two indispensable ingredients, silkworms and mulberry leaves. Though the distant origin of silk is lost in the mists of antiquity, the earliest written records are dated 1240 B.C.; its primitive beginnings undoubtedly preceded that date. From these accounts it is known that the Chinese were the first to learn that the three-thousand-foot-long thread forming the silkworm's cocoon could be wound off, spun, and woven into lustrous cloth. Legend credits the wife of an emperor with discovering the process of sericulture, and with teaching the Chinese the necessary skills. For her contribution to China's wealth and culture, she was canonized as Tsu An, "Lady of the Silkworm."

❧

For China, the production and trading of silk fibers and fabric became so important that the four-thousand-mile-long Silk Road came into being. Over it, Chinese silk traveled west, while wool, gold, and silver made its way eastward to China. Ideas, too, were exchanged;

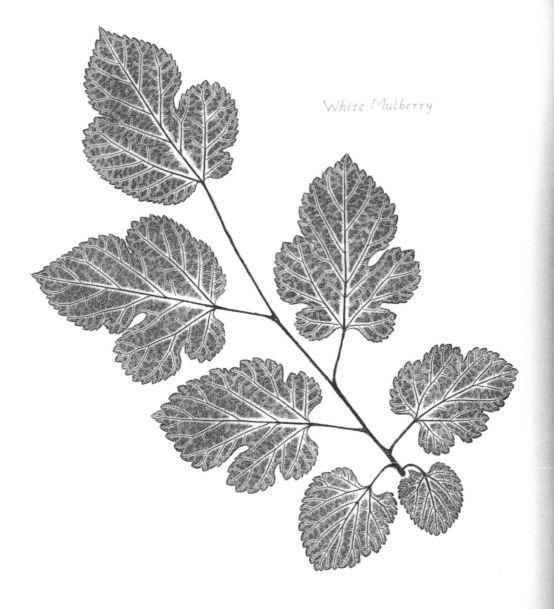

White Mulberry

Buddhism came to China from India on this celebrated highway.

In 1271 Marco Polo, the Venetian adventurer, journeyed to China over this historic route, and his book, *Travels of Marco Polo*, brought the first written account of China and its silk to the West. In his words, "Through Cathay [China] to the kingdom of Tainfu, Mulberry trees also abound which enable the inhabitants to produce large quantities of silk."

Though modern refinements have since been applied to silkworm culture, the process remains essentially the same as in antiquity. Disease-free eggs are put into cold storage to await the springtime leafing of mulberry trees. Upon hatching, the worms are constantly supplied with fresh leaves on which they feed voraciously for five weeks, consuming two hundred pounds of leaves for each pound of silk eventually produced. On reaching maturity, after growing to seventy times their original size, they spin cocoons of white or yellow fibers that later become strands of silk. The worms are then killed by heat to prevent their emergence from the cocoons, which would rupture the threads. Wound off, cleaned, twisted into thread, and woven, these filaments finally become the luxurious fabric known as silk.

Tea made from the leaves of the mulberry alleviated headaches and soothed coughs. Its fruit was eaten to improve circulation and strengthen the blood; it was even believed helpful for diabetes.

NEW JERSEY TEA

New Jersey Tea   *Ceanothus americanus*   (Buckthorn Family)

All American schoolchildren know the story of the Boston Tea Party; only a few are acquainted with another less celebrated political occurrence, the New Jersey Tea Party. It was this colorful event that gave the leaves of New Jersey Tea, a small subshrub, their brief fame in history.

※

In December 1774, the *Greyhound*, an English ship bound for Philadelphia with a cargo of tea, sailed up the Delaware River. Knowing that other tea ships going to Boston, New York, and Philadelphia had been turned back, the captain decided to unload his tea in nearby Greenwich, New Jersey, a town at the mouth of Cohansey Creek. There he knew a sympathetic Tory named Sam Bowen, who he was sure would allow the tea to be stored in his cellar. This was done as planned, but somehow the secret leaked out and the patriots responded.

※

On the night of December 22, a band of forty young revolutionaries disguised as Indians marched from Bridgeton, through Shiloh, to Greenwich, where they stormed Bowen's cellar, seized the tea, and set it on fire.

※

The English shippers initiated a court action, but American patriotic fervor was such that no jury could possibly be found that would find the patriots guilty.

※

After the Boston and New Jersey Tea Parties, English tea was patriotically boycotted. Following the example of the Native Americans, the settlers began to brew tea with the dried leaves of a local shrub, called pong-pong by the Indians and New Jersey tea by the settlers. To improve the taste, the colonists laced their beverage with milk and honey or sugar. During the Revolutionary War, New Jersey tea became the best known tea alternative of all native American plants.

※

The Native Americans also made a medicinal decoction of these leaves to heal ulcerated sore throats. And now, more than two centuries later, modern medicine has at last discovered that the New Jersey tea plant, and others of its group (*Ceanothus*) are, indeed, therapeutically valuable; specifically, they contain an element useful for increasing the coagulation of the blood.

※

New Jersey Tea

WOODY NIGHTSHADE

Woody Nightshade   *Solanum dulcamara*   (Nightshade Family)

This common, clambering Eurasian vine, now frequently seen in North American wastelands, belongs to the Nightshade family, one of the largest plant groups on earth; as such, it is related to valuable food plants: the potato, tomato, pepper, and eggplant. All parts, however, of the woody nightshade—also called poisonous nightshade or deadly nightshade —are dangerously toxic if eaten raw. Despite its evil nature, the leaves and fresh green branches have been used medicinally for centuries. Included in the *U.S. Pharmacopoeia* and the *Eclectic Materia Medica* in recent times, it was

also known in antiquity by Galen, the second-century Greek physician, who recommended this nightshade for treating cancers and other tumors, and also warts. Interestingly, recent scientific studies prove that this plant does indeed contain a tumor-inhibiting element.

✳

Between the time of Galen and the present, others, too, have believed nightshade to be healing. Gerard, the sixteenth-century English botanist, claimed that "the juice is good for those who have fallen from high places, and have been thereby bruised and beaten, for it is thought to dissolve blood congealed or cluttered in the 'intrals' [sic] and to heale hurt places."

✵

Culpeper, another English herbalist, believed it helped shingles, erysipelas, and other "hot inflammations," but rightly added this prudent warning: "It is somewhat dangerous when given inwardly, unless by a skillful hand."

✵

Mary Grieve, the respected English author of *A Modern Herbal*, in 1931, recommended woody nightshade for chronic rheumatism, advising that an infusion of one ounce of dried leaves and tender tips to one cup of water be taken in wine-glassful doses two or three times daily.

✵

American folk medicine recommended mashing the green leaves in cream until the cream turned green to make a soothing poultice for poison ivy. Confirming this country use of nightshade, chemists now say that this plant contains solanine, a substance effective for healing obstinate skin disorders and ulcers.

✵

More than simply medicinally curative, this plant supposedly possessed a healing magic. Shepherds in Germany used to treat animals suffering from *Die Hynsch*, a form of dizziness, by hanging leafy green garlands of woody nightshade around their necks.

To ease sunburn, crush a handful of nightshade leaves and twigs into a cup of light cream, stirring until cream acquires a light-green shade. Pat the solution gently onto sunburned areas. For poison ivy, crush several leaves in a cup and add a few drops of condensed milk. Apply to affected skin area.

Woody Nightshade

LIVE OAK

Live Oak   *Quercus virginiana*   (Beech Family)

The magnificent live oak is the glory of the American South. Many Americans are familiar with the image of stately plantations surrounded by moss-draped live oaks. Southern graveyards, too, are guarded by these stalwart sentinels.

❧

Short-trunked and strong-branched, the wide-spreading branches of the live oak are perennially covered with glossy, dark leaves. Its name "live oak" refers to the enduring greenness of this tree which is in stark contrast to the deciduous oaks that seasonally shed all their leaves and stand bare in winter. The green leaves of the live oak continually cover this tree because they are not cast off all at once. Leaves cling to this tree for about thirteen months and new ones are formed as the old ones fall off. However, north of Virginia where the live oaks grow rarely, they are only partially evergreen and sometimes completely deciduous.

❧

Thorough searching has uncovered none of the more ordinary folk uses for these leaves—no medicines, teas, or poisonous brews—but they have their own special claim to fame. These leaves once inspired Walt Whitman, whose poetry was a continuous celebration of his native land. He wrote:

> I saw in Louisiana a live oak growing.
> Alone stood it, and the moss hung
>   down from its branches.
> Without any companion it stood there,
>   uttering joyous leaves of dark green.

Who but Whitman would have penned that surprising and original phrase—"uttering joyous leaves."

✽

One spectacular tree of truly giant proportions, located in Hilton Park in Wilmington, North Carolina, is known as the South's Living Christmas Tree. Not the usual holiday conifer with evergreen needles, this tree is, instead, a live oak crowned yearlong with shining leaves. During the holiday season, it glows with thousands of multi-colored Christmas lights.

✽

Incredibly beautiful, the live oak is naturally adorned with several layers of pendulous gray Spanish moss (*Tillandsia usneoides*). This moss is not a true parasite but a tree-dwelling plant.

✽

Live Oak

Note: This illustration—a print of the living leaves—also shows a few strands of this pendant moss.

Of all the trees that grow so fair,
Old England to adorn,
Greater are none beneath the Sun,
Than oak, and ash, and thorn.

—Rudyard Kipling,
A Tree Song

White Oak

WHITE OAK

White Oak   *Quercus alba*   (Beech Family)

The white oak, a noble American tree, is renowned in legend and in history, and for the many uses of its timber. It once furnished the wood for barrels, barns, bridges, buildings, and the decks and keels of ships, as well as the wood for the all-oak ships that carried New England sea captains around the world.

⁂

Two splendid white oaks in New Jersey are historically famous. The first in Princeton, known as the Mercer Oak, is the tree from under which General Mercer of the Revolutionary War, though mortally wounded, bravely directed his troops, then died.

⁂

The second, a venerable giant in New Brunswick, the Kilmer Oak, is the tree that reputedly inspired Joyce Kilmer to write this famous verse:

> I think that I shall never see
> A poem lovely as a tree.

⁂

The dramatic story of another white oak—legendary in the history of Connecticut—involved a daring theft and successful defiance against British authority.

⁂

In 1687, King James II of England, in an effort to unite all the New England colonies under one government, directed Connecticut's Governor Andros to retract that state's charter, an action the

But my heart goes out to the Oak leaves
that are the last to sigh, "Enough,"
and loose their hold.

—Edna St. Vincent Millay,
Wine From These Grapes

colonists stubbornly opposed. Arriving with an armed guard in Hartford, the capital, Andros tried to coerce the dissidents, who at first even refused to bring out the charter. Finally, that evening, when it was reluctantly brought forth, candles were lit and a discussion ensued. Suddenly the candles went out and, when relit, the charter was mysteriously gone.

🌸

Joseph Wadsworth, a known thief and scoundrel, by prearrangement committed this patriotic theft, then slipped out and hid the charter in the hollow tree that later became known as the Charter Oak.

🌸

Less famous than the tree's history or its timber, the leaves have few recorded practical uses. Dried leaves steeped in hot water were once

To cure frostbite, American folk medicine called for collecting oak leaves that had remained on the tree all through the winter. These leaves were boiled to obtain a solution in which the frostbitten extremities would soak for an hour each day for a week.

A Vermont fable tells of a wealthy old man who sold his soul to the Devil in return for an extension of his life; the bargain specified that the man would enjoy his life and riches until the oak lost all its leaves. That crafty gentleman knew that the white oak is almost never bare of leaves (a few dried ones from the previous year always hang on). But when the Devil realized he had been tricked, he viciously chewed the leaves where, to this day, you can see the marks of his anger in the shape of the leaves.

recognized in country medicine for relieving chilblains, but substances in the young leaves of this tree also reputedly killed browsing cattle. Native Americans knew it was time to plant their corn in the spring when white oak leaves were "big as a mouse's ear."

The tannin found in oak can help reduce minor blistering. Boil a piece of oak bark in a small amount of water until a strong solution is reached. Apply to affected area as often as desired.

OLEANDER

Oleander   *Nerium oleander*   (Dogbane Family)

Of the many ornamental shrubs embellishing American gardens, none is more beautiful than the flowering oleander. This import from Asia Minor is cherished for its abundant clusters of rose-red, pink, or white flowers, and for its handsome evergreen leaves. For growing outdoors year-long, oleander needs a mild climate, while in cold, northern areas, it must be pampered, pot-grown, and winter-sheltered.

But oleander's beauty comes with a price, since all parts of the shrub are flawed with a poison hidden within, a poison so potent that eating a single leaf, or even a piece of grilled meat skewered with its wood, will lead to death.

In ancient Greece, according to the physician Dioscorides, the dangers of oleander were recognized: "But ye flowers and the leaves have a power destructive of dogs and asses . . . mules and most four-footed living creatures, but a preserving one of men, being drunk with wine against the bitings of venomous beasts." It is true that four-footed animals have frequently died after browsing on oleander, a fact well known in India where it is called "horse killer," but it also kills any creature that unwisely ingests any part of it.

Dioscorides' reference to oleander as a preserving power of men may have foreshadowed its use in modern medicine.

Palestinian pharma-
ceutical industries
today prepare a heart
remedy from oleander
leaves that is given to
patients with weak heart-
beats.

❦

Because of oleander's
therapeutic power, it
has had many country
uses. The juice of the
leaves relieved scabies
and mange; the bruised
leaves matured abscesses. As
a pesticide, grains of wheat
soaked in the deadly liquid of
boiled leaves swiftly killed rats and
mice. Today in Italy, people continue
to include oleander leaves in bags of
stored, dried beans to repel destructive
insects.

Oleander

OLIVE TREE

Olive Tree   *Olea europaea*   (Olive Family)

The silver-green olive tree, an enduring companion and sustainer of humans, reaches back into antiquity. Planted in biblical times, cultivated by the Egyptians, entwined with the lives of the Greeks and Romans, it is still a presence today in the lands that ring the Mediterranean. An individual tree sometimes lives for up to four centuries, becoming a green monument to the long-gone gardener who planted it. With age, the tree becomes grotesque, the trunk growing hollow, dividing into crooked legs on which it treads a slow, macabre dance through the centuries.

*

The small fruits of this ancient tree are the principal reason for its cultivation.

Dried, or preserved in brine or oil, olives are a nourishing food, a staple in Mediterranean countries. It is, however, for the green-gold oil pressed from this fruit that ninety-five percent of all olives are harvested. Prized in Homer's time for anointing the body, it was also used, then as now, to enhance food and as an aid in cooking. This fruitful tree's beautiful wood, banded dark and light and resistant to decay, is prized for carving and turnery.

*

The earliest written mention of its gray-green leaves comes from the biblical story of the flood, in the book of Genesis: "And the dove came in to him in the evening, and lo, in her mouth was an olive leaf pluckt off; so Noah knew the waters were abated from off the earth."

⁕

Since that time olive leaves have been a symbol of beneficence. To the Greeks they were a mark of peace and victory; olive leaves crowned the winners of Olympic games. And as a symbol, the words "To extend the olive branch" signify an offering as a token of peace; in this spirit two leafy olive branches appear on the banner of the United Nations.

⁕

Olive leaves have never been as appreciated as the fruit, oil, or wood, but ancient medicine did find them useful because their therapeutic astringency cleansed ulcers and reduced inflammation.

Dioscorides said, "Being applied with honey, they agglutinate the skin rent from the head," and, "They are good for the erosion of the eye-lidds." Gerard, too, declared them cooling and binding, adding: "Being chewed, they are a remedy for ulcers in the mouth."

⁕

In *A Modern Herbal* (1931), Mary Grieve maintained that olive leaves were astringent and antiseptic, and that drinking a decoction of them was effective against fever.

Olive Tree

Note: Because papaya leaves are huge—up to two feet across—only a small, young leaf is shown here.

Papaya

PAPAYA

Papaya   *Carica papaya*   (Papaya Family)

The papaya is "a clown of a tree, but very useful," claimed Liberty Hyde Bailey, a distinguished American botanist and horticulturist. Because it is unbranched and its trunk is not as woody as a typical tree, some have called it a succulent tree, while others maintain that it is a treelike herb. No one, however, disputes its usefulness, first and foremost for its oblong, golden fruit, which is smooth, juicy, and refreshingly sweet with a musky tang.

❀

Within its unripe fruit and leaves is an almost magical enzyme called papain that is capable of breaking down proteins during digestion. Country folk living where papayas grow have long used the leaves in practical ways. The Chinese claim that merely hanging a tough chicken in a papaya tree just below the leaves has a remarkable softening effect on the flesh, while Hawaiians say that cheap cuts of meat become tender and digestible when wrapped in papaya leaves and refrigerated for a few days. Papain is now used in commercial meat-tenderizers.

❀

In herbal medicine dried papaya leaves have long been used in making a tea for settling an upset stomach. (A tablespoon of dry leaves in two cups of boiling water is the recommended proportion.) Scientific medicine wisely prescribes remedies containing papain to treat impaired digestion and chronic dyspepsia.

❀

PARTRIDGEBERRY

Partridgeberry   *Mitchella repens*   (Madder Family)

The partridgeberry, an ever-green, ground-hugging vine forming a flat, green mat on the forest floor, has many names. Its flowers, fruit, leaves, and early medicinal use have all contributed to its naming.

*

Growing in pairs along slender stems, the fragrant white flowers give it the obvious title of twin flower. The names partridgeberry and deerberry signify that birds and beasts enjoy its small fruit, even though most people consider it edible but tasteless.

*

Another name explains a rather unusual botanical characteristic. Because the paired flowers share one common ovary at their base, it takes two flowers to pro-duce only one berry. The odd origin of this fruit, marked by the two small residual dots on the berry's red surface, give it the name of two-eyed berry.

*

It is also commonly called checkerberry, from the checked appearance of the whole plant with its red berries scat-tered here and there among the small, dark leaves. And "running box" likens the leaves of this ground-creeping vine to those of the upright evergreen shrub called box.

*

Finally two others, squaw berry and squaw vine, indicate that the Penobscot Native American women of Maine and the eastern Cherokees drank a therapeu-tic potion of these leaves, stems, and berries for a few weeks before giving birth to strengthen them and hasten labor, thus making childbirth easier.

✻

Partridgeberry leaves have also had their day in modern scientific medicine. From 1926 to 1947, the *U.S. National Formulary* recommended a tea of partridgeberry leaves as an effective astringent and diuretic.

✻

Partridgeberry is no longer considered healing either in scientific or herbal folk medicine, but windowsill gardeners value this slightly woody vine. Its diminutive size, small evergreen leaves, and scarlet berries make it a favorite plant for indoor winter terrariums.

Partridgeberry

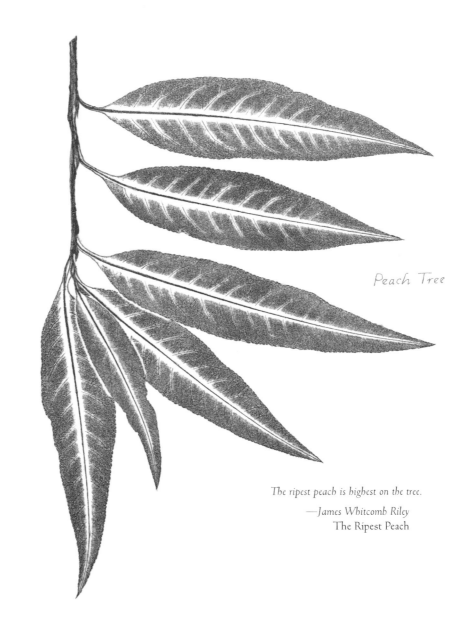

Peach Tree

The ripest peach is highest on the tree.
—James Whitcomb Riley
The Ripest Peach

PEACH TREE

Peach Tree   *Prunus persica*   (Rose Family)

The fuzzy, juicy peach is one of our most precious gifts from ancient China. Wending its way across Asia in the packs of travelers, it was named persica in Persia, now Iran. When it reached the Mediterranean countries of Europe, the Romans called it the Persian apple. Later the Spanish conquistadors brought the fruit to Mexico, where it was grown as early as 1600. Soon it traveled north with the Spanish adventurers into the territory now called the United States, where it is truly considered a queen among fruits. Today it grows worldwide wherever the climate and soil are favorable.

❋

A quotation from the Old Testament (Ezekiel 47:12) might almost have been written with the peach tree in mind: "And the fruit thereof shall be for meat [food], and the leaf thereof for medicine." There are very few leaves with recorded healing properties that have been used for so many ills by so many people as those of the small peach tree.

❋

John Gerard, the English herbalist, claimed, "The leaves of the peach tree so open the stoppings of the liver, and do gently loosen the belly; being applied unto the navell of young children, they kill worms and drive them forth."

❋

In American folk medicine, too, the idea of applying leaves externally for internal ills is frequently encountered. Native Americans crushed peach leaves into a poultice to reduce swelling, inflammation, boils, and "risings." Similarly, the Appalachian mountain people wrapped crushed peach leaves in cloth, laying the cloth on the stomach to stop vomiting and tying it around the head to calm headaches.

The list of peach leaves in therapeutic decoctions is long and varied; they have been used as a sedative, expectorant, diuretic, purgative, for bladder trouble, and also for curing jaundice. It was once even claimed that peach-leaf tea was more effective than quinine for malaria.

The American Shakers recommended peach-leaf tea for some of these same disorders—as a vermifuge, tonic, and laxative, for irritability of the bladder and inflammation of the stomach.

It can, in fact, be said that someone, somewhere, at some time has used these remarkable leaves for almost every human ill. And with so much evidence in their favor, there may be at least some curative validity.

PERSIMMON

American Persimmon   *Diospyros virginiana*   (Ebony Family)

Any American living where this tree grows knows its fruit, the mouth-puckering persimmon. Captain John Smith of the Virginia Colony correctly observed, "If it be not ripe, it will draw a man's mouth a-wry in much torment." When completely mature, however, the fruit of this native tree is meltingly sweet with a distinctive flavor, especially after it has been lightly touched with frost.

✱

Because of the persimmon's sweetness and delicious taste, the Native Americans ate it fresh, cooked, and dried, and also combined it with pounded maize to create a bread they called stan-inca. Early country Americans made persimmons into syrup, pudding, vinegar, and even beer. During the Civil War the large seeds within this edible fruit were boiled or roasted, then ground and brewed into a substitute coffee.

✱

Since the persimmon tree belongs to the Ebony family, it is not surprising that its wood is dense, heavy, and hard, with a dark, almost black heartwood that has been fashioned—among other things—into golf clubs and billiard cues.

✱

While the fruit might seem to be this tree's most valuable part, the leaves assumed a new impor-tance in 1942, when two scientists—C. G. Vinson of the University of Virginia and

Persimmon fruit is rich in potassium and high in vitamin C. For a simple dessert, cut off and discard the tops of ripe persimmons and sprinkle with sugar. Top with some cherry or orange brandy and serve.

F. B. Cross of Oklahoma's A & M College—published the findings of their joint experiments. These tests proved that persimmon leaves, especially dried ones, have an exceptionally high vitamin C content. Even more unusual, the concentration of the vitamin in the leaves is ten times higher than that of the fruit.

❧

The rich source of vitamins from the persimmon has never been commercially exploited, but those with access to the leaves can easily prepare a tea with them. Place a half cup of

dried leaves in four cups of water; bring to a boil and cook over medium heat for ten minutes. Strain and, if desired, sweeten with honey or sugar for a healthy, pleasant-tasting beverage slightly reminiscent of sassafras tea.

❧

To prepare fresh leaves for long-term storage, spread them out on newspaper until dry, then pack them in open jars. Place jars in an oven set at low heat and remove them after thirty minutes. Place lids on jars while still hot to seal thoroughly. The leaves will be usable for one year.

❧

Nurseries now sell improved fruiting varieties of this interesting, vitamin-rich, native American plant.

❧

American Persimmon

SLASH PINE

Slash Pine   *Pinus elliottii*   (Pine Family)

The slash pine is a tall, native, evergreen tree that flourishes in the American south. A slash is a low, moist, open place in the forest that is strewn with natural debris and fallen trees, victims of fire, storm, or human destruction. This pine, the fastest growing of all eastern forest trees, is usually the first to take over, healing and reforesting the damaged area, and from this helpful habit, it earned its apt name.

⁂

This pine has slender needles that range from six to twelve inches in length. Because of their practical length, strength, and pliability, they were woven into baskets by Native Americans and early settlers. Even today craftspeople

still value these needles, alone or with other natural fibers, to create baskets that are long-lasting, useful, beautiful, and pine-scented.

⁂

In the past pine needles had other practical applications. A United States government bulletin issued in 1897 listed various types of rough textiles made from long, strong pine needles, including a close-woven and durable carpet, similar to coco matting. Early upholsterers employed the cellular tissue of the needles in the manufacture of pine wool, which was used as filling material and thought to have potential as an antiseptic dressing for wounds. Though none of these early attempts have survived, in rural areas pine needles, locally called pine straw, still cover potato beds and strawberry patches as protective, moisture-preserving mulch, and animals in their stalls are sometimes bedded down on them.

❧

Pine oil, derived from fresh pine needles by a process known as destructive distillation, is still considered a valuable ingredient in antiseptic solutions such as cough medicines and expectorants, though sometimes it is replaced by a synthetic substitute.

❧

Recent scientific investigation in Germany has revealed that fresh pine needles are an excellent source of vitamin K, which is important for increasing coagulants in the blood.

❧

Yet this at least I find is surely mine
After a long hard journey and mighty cities seen
The pure sweet scent of a southern long-leafed pine
Into my nostrils breathed, soft rich and clean.

—John Gould Fletcher

Slash Pine

~ 229 ~

EASTERN
WHITE PINE

Eastern White Pine   *Pinus strobus*   (Pine Family)

More than any other tree, the white pine—king of all native pines—built America. Because the light, strong wood is easy to work with and finishes well, it was, for three hundred years, the favorite wood of carpenters; as such it was the most common timber used for homes, churches, mills, barns, and bridges. The towering height and straight form of the trunks marked them also as the prime source of masts for America's early wooden sailing ships. Today, because of extensive lumbering, only a few such giant white pines still stand, trees that once reached heights of two hundred feet or more.

The needles of the white pine differentiate it from all other native eastern pines, as it is the only one whose needles grow in bundles of five, one for each letter of the word "white."

Perhaps because their resinous fragrance hinted at a possible medicinal value, pine needles once captured the imagination of country folk, who drank strong pine tea several times a day as a remedy for coughs, and at bedtime to induce perspiration and benefit colds. For preventing or treating scurvy—a frequent problem during colonial times—the Native Americans of New England drank an infusion made from young needles gathered in spring. Even

White Pine

Sweet is the whispering music of
yonder pine that sings.

—*Theocritus*

Because it was an easy wood to work with, eastern white pine was considered valuable. The British Crown at one time ordered colonists to set aside white pine to be used for the masts of the Royal Navy. This so outraged the colonists that they would steal the trees back under cover of night.

today, in the Ramapo Hills of New Jersey, the mountain people still claim that a whiskey glass filled with this beverage, hot and strong, helps arthritis.

❋

According to recent scientific analysis, fresh needles are exceptionally rich in vitamin A and especially vitamin C; it has been estimated that a cupful of strong pine-needle tea has more vitamin C than the average lemon.

❋

The resinous fragrance of pine is undeniably pleasant, but for the Chinese, it was even more—it was vital. They fumigated their houses with these nee-dles, to aid, they said, in the expulsion of "evil spirits." Native Americans sweetened the air of their homes by placing dried needles in open jars, and for their soporific effect, they laid bags of needles near the heads of those who couldn't sleep. Even today, country housekeepers still claim that the spicy aroma of pine needles in chests or closets protects woolens from destructive moths.

❋

About these remarkable needles, there is one final thought to ponder. A small but important bit of ancient Chinese wisdom warns: "It is more difficult to win love than to wrap salt in pine needles."

Sometimes I rambled in Pine groves, standing like temples, or like fleets at sea, full rigged with wavy boughs.

—Henry David Thoreau, Journals, Vol.II

UMBRELLA PINE

Umbrella Pine   *Sciadopitys verticillata*   (Taxodium Family)

A tall, slender pyramid, the evergreen umbrella pine is a sacred tree in Japan. There, during ancient feudal times, it was one of the "Five Trees of Kiso"—five majestic trees selected as the best, most beautiful, and most valuable in that country. Today it is also honored as the traditional decoration during the popular Japanese festival of Bon.

This Buddhist holiday celebrated for three days in mid-July is solemn but also joyous, because at this time the dead are said to return in spirit to their birthplace to visit with their living relatives. It is a festival of lights; paper lanterns and fires are lit to welcome the dead. Joyful community dances are performed, and invocations, prayers, and chants are spoken to honor and express gratitude toward the spirits, perpetuate their memories, and strengthen the ties between the living and dead family members. Buddhist graveyards are cleaned, and symbolizing undying love and respect, branches of evergreen umbrella pine, with their unusual whorled leaves, are placed on the memorial stones. At the festival's end, lights once again illuminate the way of the spirits' return voyage to their other world.

This respected tree, growing slowly to more than one hundred feet, is native to only two islands of Japan, Shikoku and southern Honshu. Though it is commonly named pine, it is, in reality, only a most distant relative, in fact one so remote that time has obliterated all traces of its immediate ancestors. Botanists claim that it is one of the oldest living species of plants. The whorled, spokelike needles give it the descriptive name of umbrella pine.

*

The needles are unusual not only in their arrangement on the twigs but in their construction as well. Botanical morphologists—scientists who concern themselves with the form and construction of plants—claim that each of the needles is, in reality, two needles that eons ago fused themselves into one.

*

In some distant geologic era, umbrella pines were so prolific in Japan, and their leaf-fall so prodigious, that the fallen leaves, under pressure beneath the earth's crust, formed a layer of carbon known today as grass coal. By observing the form of the living needles, one can see the probable reason for the name of this coal.

*

This beautiful, ancient tree was introduced into America in 1862, but it is still only minimally known. For its unique beauty, its unusual circling leaves, and also the surrounding aura of its history, it deserves more popular appreciation.

*

To cure bronchitis, an old gypsy remedy calls for mixing together 1 teaspoon of pine resin, 1 drop of essential lavender oil, and 1 tablespoon of honey into a glass of warm milk. Drink one glass of this three times per day.

Umbrella Pine

COMMON PLUM

Common Plum   *Prunus x domestica*   (Rose Family)

The plum tree, a drift of snowy white, is among the first trees to burst into bloom in the waning days of winter. This untimely blossoming led the Chinese of the Ming Dynasty to match it with the cold-defying pine and the chill-enduring bamboo and then name the trio the "Three Friends of Winter," immortalizing all three on exquisite blue-and-white porcelain.

✻

But the plum is more than just a lovely flowering tree. After the blossoms fade,

it bears in its season an abundant crop of sweet, purple-blue fruit from which the Chinese concoct their famous plum sauce, an essential ingredient in their cuisine. In the West, plums are eaten fresh, dried as prunes, canned, or made into jam. In Germany, they are the key ingredients in delicious plum *küchen*, while Yugoslavia celebrates the plum with the fiery liquor called *slivowitz*.

✻

This fruitful tree also bears healing leaves that ancient medicine used to cure infections of the mouth and throat. As Dioscorides wrote in his renowned herbal, "Ye decoctions of plum leaves ordered or prepared in wine doth stop the flux that falls upon the Uva, the Gingivae and ye tonsillae."

✻

Many centuries later, John Gerard, the

English herbalist, kept the ancient ideas of Dioscorides alive when he echoed the same advice, though in a wordier style: "The leaves of the plum tree are good against the swellings of the uvula [soft palate] the throat, gums and kernels under the throat and jaws. They stop the rheume and falling down of humors if the decoction thereof be made in wine and gargled in the mouth and throat."

The Native Americans also prepared a therapeutic mouthwash from plum leaves. The centuries-old use of these leaves for the same disorders argues a certain validity.

Although plum leaves as a remedy for inflamed throats have been usurped by the advanced remedies of modern medicine, craftspeople continue to use them to make subtle shades of green to dye yarn and fabric.

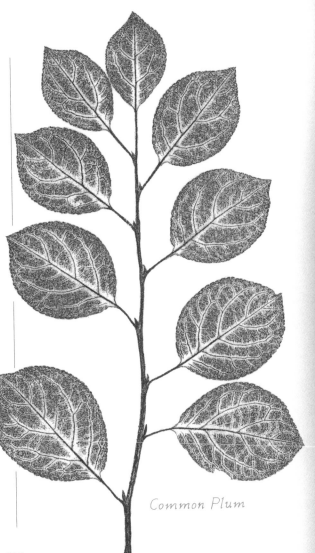

Common Plum

POINSETTIA

Poinsettia *Euphorbia pulcherrima* (Spurge Family)

When is a flower not a flower? The answer to that botanical riddle: when it's a poinsettia. The scarlet starburst, so much a part of the American Christmas tradition, is in reality a whorl of brilliant floral leaves, or bracts, surrounding the true flowers, the small, central, knoblike structures.

❧

Indigenous to Mexico and probably Guatemala, this striking shrub was introduced into the United States by Joel Roberts Poinsett, linguist, scientist,

horticulturist, and the controversial nineteenth-century American minister to Mexico. In his honor this handsome plant was later named for him. In warm areas, such as Florida, California, and its native Mexico, it grows outdoors as a fifteen-foot shrub, while in the colder north, it is small, pot-grown, and winter-sheltered.

❧

Unfortunately, though bright and beautiful, the poinsettia, a member of the poisonous Spurge family, is somewhat toxic in all its parts, and—at the very least—irritating when taken internally; ingested by young children, it can be seriously dangerous.

❧

Though the poinsettia has always been known as an irritant, in Mexico a decoction of the red floral leaves—five grams in five hundred grams of water—was at one time prescribed to nursing mothers to increase their milk. Large doses, however, were considered hazardous for both mother and child.

✳

This charming legend comes from Mexico: A small boy had no gift to place before the crèche in the church, the traditional Mexican custom, so he knelt outside to pray. Miraculously, where he bent in prayer, a beautiful plant with scarlet, starlike "flowers" appeared. Because the whorled red "petals" resembled the star of Bethlehem, the boy proudly presented this plant as his gift to the Holy Child, thus earning the poinsettia its Mexican name, *Flor de la Noche Buena*, or "Flower of the Holy Night."

Poinsettia

Poison Ivy

POISON IVY

Poison Ivy   *Rhus radicans*   (Cashew Family)

Leaflets three,
Let them be.

❀

So runs the childhood chant that warns against the noxious poison ivy. While many Americans are painfully familiar with this irritating New World plant, it is unknown in Europe except as a specimen in botanical gardens.

❀

In 1624 Captain John Smith, the English founder of the Virginia Colony, observed this plant and wrote, "It causeth rednesse; itching and lastly blisters…which howsoever, after a while passe away of themselves without further harme." What he failed to describe is the agony endured between the first "rednesse" and the time the blisters "passe away of themselves."

❀

Numerous legends surround this plant of evil repute. The Cherokees, when working near poison ivy, attempted to conciliate it by addressing it as "my friend"; while a common folk belief claimed that anyone even looking at it in wet weather would be poisoned by it.

❀

So-called cures and ways of lessening its effects abound. Native Americans, lumberjacks, and other outdoor people have claimed that eating the leaves confers absolute immunity. There is one story on record of a man who not only ate the leaves himself, but each spring fed them to his wife and five children who reportedly suffered no ill effects. In contrast, two reputable botanists, in a bulletin from the University of Minnesota, emphatically warned, "Under no circumstances should you eat a leaf in the mistaken notion that this will promote immunity—severe gastric irritation can result."

❋

The violent irritant, hydro-urushiol, an oil present in all its plant parts except the pollen and the leaf hairs, is responsible for the unbearable dermatitis (skin inflammation). Washing the skin thoroughly within minutes after contact may lessen the severity, but it will not cure the irritation completely.

❋

In spite of poison ivy's evil reputation, it also has beneficent uses. Native Americans mashed the leaves into a poultice for treating ringworm, and they brewed a rejuvenating tea from the leaves. The Shakers recommended these leaves as a counterirritant for rheumatism, paralysis of the bladder, and also for skin disorders. Practitioners of homeopathic medicine once prescribed a tincture of leaves for eruptive skin diseases. And from 1820 to 1905, poison ivy was listed in the *U.S. Pharmacopoeia* as a nerve sedative and as a treatment for acute rheumatism and painful stiffness of the joints.

❋

Though at times poison ivy has been beneficial, total avoidance of this plant is still strongly recommended.

Poison ivy leaves are used by some people as a homeopathic remedy for the pain of rheumatism. A tincture is made from the pulverized leaves which have been taken from the plant prior to its flowering, a time when the poison is most potent.

COMMON PRIVET

Common Privet   *Ligustrum vulgare*   (Olive Family)

rivet is a versatile shrub with an ancient history. Five centuries before Christ, so legend relates, Anacreon, the Greek poet, ornamentally wreathed his seven-stringed lyre with privet while he chanted his erotic verses.

❧

In the more recent past, Victorian gardeners delighted in the decorative privet for topiary work, clipping and carving this close-leaved shrub into fantastic green sculpture—swans, rabbits, bears, even unknown and mythical beasts.

❧

In formal European gardens this artistic, creative cutting continues, but in America today, privet has become, instead, a practical choice for space-defining hedges. And because many gardeners keep their hedges so precisely trimmed they miss out on the scented clusters of white blossoms that this plant can produce; the flowers, sadly, are prematurely nipped in the bud.

❧

Pliny, the Roman naturalist, speaking of privet, confidently declared, "Its leaves everywhere are used to treat ulcers, and with a sprinkling of salt, sores in the mouth." In sixteenth-century England, John Gerard echoed this old wisdom: "The leaves of privet do cure the swellings of the mouth or throat being gargarified with the juyce or decoction thereof." Later

Common Privet

in nineteenth-century America the herb-gathering Shakers sold these leaves as an antiscurvy medicine, and, as in antiquity, as an astringent, healing mouthwash.

✳

Though these therapeutic uses occurred before the age of modern scientific medicine, these early healers were unequivocally right. Scientists have now affirmed that the leaves of some species of privet contain sufficient antibiotics to stop the action of the dangerous pus-forming bacteria called *staphylococcus aurea*, which is responsible for many infections.

✳

Authentic medicinal plants given in careful doses are effective for healing, but frequently these same plants are also toxic. Sheep, horses, and cattle have suffered gastric irritation, vomiting, severe pain, even death after feeding on privet hedges.

✳

Today craftspeople use privet leaves as a dye. Depending on the mordants, leaves can yield shades of color ranging from pale yellow to deep green.

RASPBERRY BUSH

American Red Raspberry   *Rubus idaeus var. strigosus*   (Rose Family)

The bristly American raspberry shrub, which grows in the cool northern reaches of the United States, is the bearer of fragrant, thimblelike red berries. Perhaps because of their perishable nature, only small quantities of these soft, sweet berries appear in commercial markets. Though they are delicious when eaten fresh or in pies and jam, people often object to their many seeds, so they are strained and made into jelly.

❧

In the past, Native American women drank raspberry-leaf tea throughout their term of pregnancy. During labor, they would drink a hot, stronger version to quicken and ease the birthing process. Colonial midwives followed their lead and routinely gave this fortifying tea to their patients.

❧

Many years later, during World War II, fragarine, the active ingredient in raspberry leaves, was finally "discovered" by obstetricians as a relaxant of the uterine muscles—an aid in childbirth—thus confirming the early Native American knowledge.

❧

Decoctions of these astringent, tannin-laden leaves were once consid-

To treat diarrhea, steep 1 to 2 teaspoons of dried raspberry leaves in 1 cup of boiling water for 10 to 15 minutes. Drink as needed.

Red Raspberry

ered the most effective home remedy for diarrhea (especially in children), and were also given as diuretics as well as for controlling nausea associated with vomiting. It was also once commonly believed that this potent tea used as a mouthwash would dissolve tartar on the teeth and heal mouth sores.

✻

John Gerard, the English herbalist, had something still more unusual to say about raspberry leaves. Calling this plant the "raspis," he claimed that its leaves, as well as those of the related blackberry, "Heale the eyes that hang out."

✻

Quite aside from its therapeutic use, raspberry-leaf tea is a pleasant beverage. Taken in reasonable quantities and made from thoroughly dried leaves, it is safe and wholesome. It is important to remember, however, that raspberry leaves containing moisture also contain hydrocyanic acid, a dangerous poison.

✻

Wilted (but not thoroughly dried) raspberry leaves included in uncured hay are also a danger to cattle, sometimes even causing death, while leaves in fully dried hay produce no ill effects. And though never mentioned today, the foliage and young shoots of the raspberry were once an established remedy for infertility in bulls and stallions.

RASPBERRY FRUIT DRINK

4 cups of raspberries
3-1/4 cups sugar.
3/4 cup white vinegar
1 cup water

Combine ingredients and let stand until berries release their juice. Simmer for 10 to 12 minutes, remove from heat, and cool. Strain and add water or seltzer to taste. Serve over ice.

CATAWBA RHODODENDRON

Catawba Rhododendron   *Rhododendron catawbiense*   (Heath Family)

When the rhododendrons are in bloom in spring and early summer, flower lovers everywhere make their annual pilgrimages into the Blue Ridge and Great Smoky Mountains of the American South to witness their splendid color. The opulent flower clusters of the catawba rhododendron cover the shrubs with a blanket of lilac or white, while its larger relative, the great rhododendron, blooms in shades of pink, rose, and even dark red.

❦

Unfortunately, these exquisite blossoms contain a toxic nectar, the source of poisonous honey that careful Appalachian beekeepers routinely destroy.

❦

Year-round the slopes of the Blue Ridge and Great Smoky Mountains are covered with impenetrable rhododendron thickets known locally as "green hells." So dense is this evergreen foliage that, according to folk legend, rhododendrons

To preserve these leaves for long-lasting winter bouquets, select branches about eighteen inches long with perfect leaves; wash and dry them well, then pound the bottom five inches of wood with a hammer. Immediately place the stems into a tall, narrow container filled with a solution of one-third glycerine to two-thirds water. Replenish water as it evaporates, but add no more glycerine. Repeat until color of leaves changes to their tips. The leaves will turn bronze-green in about two weeks and will keep indefinitely.

have hidden the illegal stills of mountain moonshiners for generations.

❧

Rhododendrons are among the most admired shrubs for parks and home gardens. Because they grow very slowly and live a long time, they are a favorite among gardeners.

❧

The dark, leathery leaves of the rhododendron were also once used to treat rheumatism and gout, though they were never a popular remedy because they contain a very dangerous poison called andromedotoxin. (Sheep or cattle that eat these leaves when other forage is scarce can die, though wild deer have been observed eating small quantities with no apparent harm.)

Catawba Rhododendron

ROSEMARY

Rosemary   *Rosmarinus officinalis*   (Mint Family)

More than any other shrub in this great green world, the scented plant poetically named rosemary has made itself dear to humans. It has earned this enduring esteem because of its enticing aroma, a fragrance so powerful it inspired Linnaeus to say, "In Spain where it grows abundantly, sailors, even before they can see land, are refreshed by its odor." The fragrant oil in the leaves is the source of its remarkable perfume and its legendary status in superstitions, traditions, medicine, and food.

✿

In the ancient world rosemary was considered an aid to memory, and to benefit from its powers, Greek students twined it hopefully in their hair before examinations. Ancient Arab physicians agreed that "rosemary comforteth the brains and the memory." And everyone who has read *Hamlet* knows Ophelia's famous line: "There's rosemary, that's for remembrance." Rosemary tea made from leaves crushed in wine was once a home remedy for restoring lost memory, or at least for strengthening the ability to remember. And even in England today rosemary wreaths are laid on soldiers' graves so all will recall their heroic deeds.

✿

Scented rosemary was also the chosen herb for the preservation of youthful beauty, especially of hair and skin. A sixteenth-century prescription advised, "Seethe much rosemary, and bathe therein, to make thee lusty, lively, youthful and youngly." A legend tells of its rejuvenating power on an old, wrinkled queen: "Of rosemary she took six pownde, ground it well in a stownde," bathed three times a day, anointed her head with the "goode balm," and became young again.

🐝

Since rosemary was believed to bring success to any undertaking, it was popular for bestowing among friends. Small sprigs inserted into a bridal bouquet ensured a happy marriage.

🐝

But fabled rosemary's greatest acclaim came from its use in early medicine, where its leaves were almost a complete pharmacy by themselves, a cure for headaches, sore eyes, fevers, colds, heart disease, nausea, jaundice, rheumatism, gout, faulty digestion, and drunkenness; all were treated with baths, teas, fumes, and poultices of leaves. Even as recently as World War I, rosemary was burned in French hospital wards to prevent the spread of infection. Though belief in these extravagant claims has vanished, rosemary is used today as a culinary herb for flavoring meat, broiled fish, and especially roast chicken.

Legend tells of a hermit who provided Queen Elizabeth of Hungary with a cure for her paralysis. He soaked a pound of rosemary in a gallon of wine for several days, after which he applied the solution to her limbs. Upon hearing of the queen's miraculous recovery, the solution was dubbed Queen Hungary's Water and became popular as a treatment for skin problems, baldness, gout, and dandruff.

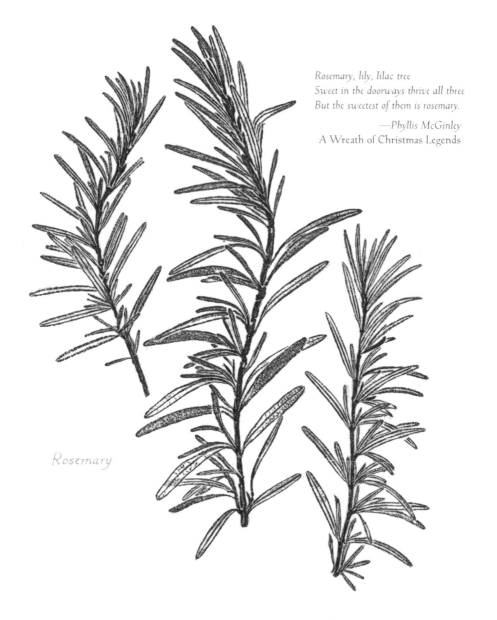

Rosemary, lily, lilac tree
Sweet in the doorways thrive all three
But the sweetest of them is rosemary.

—Phyllis McGinley
A Wreath of Christmas Legends

Rosemary

RUBBER TREE

India Rubber Tree   *Ficus elastica*   (Mulberry Family)

In the hot, humid forests of Asia, the India rubber tree, thick with lustrous evergreen leaves, grows high and handsome. Once extensively cultivated in Assam, Nepal, and Burma as an abundant source of natural rubber, this tree has lost much of its past importance because of the recent development of synthetic rubber substitutes. This noble tree also flourished as an ornamental, a species introduced into the warmest parts of Florida, where it lends its large-leaved, exotic elegance to palms and other tropical trees.

❧

Americans from the colder parts of the country know it only as an ornamental potted plant during its juvenile stage. The beauty of its shiny, dark leaves and their long-lasting durability under difficult indoor conditions account for the rubber tree's perennial popularity.

❧

Angel wings, the skeletonized, bleached leaves of the rubber tree, make a most unusual home decoration. Though gauzy and delicate, these treated and dried leaves are enduring and can be used alone or with other natural materials for winter bouquets. The process of creating them is messy and malodorous, but the results are worth the effort.

❧

To create angel wings, you must first skeletonize the leaves (expose their fragile network of veins), then bleach them. To begin, lay separate leaves, detached from their branches, in a large receptacle of water for two to three weeks. Then, place them in a separate basin of clean water and very gently rub off with the fingers the now-softened green substance, which will expose the fine veins. Do this with the utmost caution to avoid breaking the delicate network. Rinse the leaves carefully but thoroughly in clean water and dry each one between paper towels.

For the pale, ethereal look that gives them the right to the name angel wings, the leaves must next be whitened. In a glass jar, combine one tablespoon of laundry bleach with one quart of water. Immerse one leaf at a time into this solution, cover the jar, and watch carefully to obtain the degree of whiteness desired. Remember that over-bleaching can cause brittleness. Upon removing the leaves from the bleaching liquid, dry and flatten them between paper towels. When all of the leaves are thoroughly dry, fashion a spray of decorative angel wings by unobtrusively wiring several leaves by their short stems to an attractive, bare branch.

Rubber Tree

Sage

SAGE

Sage   *Salvia officinalis*   (Mint Family)

The small gray-green sage, a modest subshrub with aromatic leaves, was one of the most important herbs of antiquity. Native to the Mediterranean world, it was known as a multifaceted medicinal capable of coping with an endless variety of health problems. If old proverbs can be believed, sage was even able to conquer death.

*

"Why," queried one Latin adage, "should a man die who grows sage in his garden?" Also linking sage with immortality, an English couplet declared:

He who would live for aye,
Must eat Sage in the month of May.

*

Even as late as 1699, John Evelyn, an English author and naturalist wrote, "Tis a plant endued with so many wonderful properties, that the assiduous use of it is said to render man immortal."

*

And though not promising everlasting life, another herbalist declared that infusions of sage leaves would make a person immune from "the ill effects of old age," and would enable him to enjoy "full muscular strength, brightness of vision and youthful appearance all of his days."

*

Others credited sage, in teas, decoctions, compresses, and inhalations, with almost universal healing power, believing it strengthened the brain, helped the memory, and cured nervous disorders.

Its purifying power, they claimed, detoxified the liver and the kidneys and removed stones from the gallbladder; it also benefited coughs, colds, and asthma, and healed infections of the mouth  and throat. For truly serious problems, such as heart, epilepsy, and pregnancy, as well as for minor disorders such as sunburn, worms, gray hair, and stained teeth, sage was the sovereign remedy. It was a reliable antidote against "the bitings of serpents." And for that most grievous of maladies, the sorrow caused by the death of a loved one, sage was a comforting cure.

※

For lack of substantial proof, the attractive claims of immortality must be discounted, but some of sage's other curative powers were once taken seriously enough for this plant to be included in the official pharmacopoeias of the United States, England, Austria, and Italy.

※

Today, though its medical stature is diminished, its culinary importance as a flavor enhancer lives on. Its uses in poultry stuffings, pork dressings, veal dishes, and sausage are well known by cooks in many countries: the English even favor its flavor in cheese. And sage tea remains a gentle and pleasant beverage.

Sage is a natural and effective insect repellent. Plant it near other garden vegetables to protect them against insect attack.

Sagebrush

SAGEBRUSH

Sagebrush   *Artemisia tridentata*   (Composite Family)

The silvery sagebrush of the American West is a plant of mystery. From where did it come and when? Botanists who specialize in the origins of plants are unsure. Some believe it to be native to America, while others claim it came from a distant but unnamed place, and that it was introduced into the West around 1881 and became abundantly naturalized. Whatever its history, this small, vigorous shrub with spicy, gray-green leaves now blankets vast stretches of the high, dry, alkaline plains of western America.

Sagebrush belongs to a large plant group of bitter aromatic herbs and shrubs whose leaves have proven therapeutic properties. Native Americans of the West knew its remarkable healing powers, and for them the leaves were a complete living pharmacy. The Hopis, calling it *wi kwapi*, said, "It is really good for everything," and the long list of ailments treated with these all-healing leaves corroborates this enthusiastic claim.

The curative hot tea brewed from the leaves for influenza, colds, and fevers was only the merest beginning of the virtues of this multipowered medicinal. It was also effective for diarrhea, menstrual difficulties, as a strength-giving tonic after childbirth, for easing asthma, to promote the flow of urine, as an antidote against poison, and also for ridding children of worms.

※

The leaves themselves were chewed for the relief of indigestion and flatulence, while copious additions of boiled leaves in bath water mitigated the pain of rheumatism, sprains, and sore muscles.

※

Branches of foliage were burned on open fires, and the smoke inhaled opened clogged nasal passages. In addition, the fragrant fumes cleansed and fumigated the air of rooms where infectious illnesses had been endured and purified the air of birthing rooms. A strong decoction of leaves disinfected cuts and bullet wounds, safely bathed newborns, and, as a wholesome shampoo, kept the hair shiny and the scalp healthy. The expressed juice of the leaves, or the dried leaves powdered, when sprinkled on obstinate sores,

hastened their healing. The all but endless list continues, to include—as the Hopis once believed—almost "everything."

※

And for other inhabitants of the arid western plains, such as jackrabbits, hares, pronghorn antelopes, and other wildlife, this beneficent plant is an evergreen, life-sustaining source of nourishment.

※

His first consciousness was a sense of the light dry wind blowing in through the windows, with the fragrance of hot sun and sagebrush and sweet clover; a wind that made one's body feel light and one's heart cry "To-day, to-day," like a child's.

—Willa Cather,
Death Comes for the Archbishop

SALAL

Salal   *Gaultheria shallon*   (Heath Family)

Klkwsala—this is the tongue-twisting name the Chinook Indians of the Northwest gave this native shrub, an evergreen plant growing exclusively in coastal regions from Alaska to Southern California. The Chinooks brewed its leaves to make a tea that was both a refreshing beverage with a piquant, acidic flavor, and a medicine. In addition, they smoked the dried leaves as tobacco, usually combining them with other leaves, such as bearberry.

Simplifying and shortening *klkwsala*, Americans now call this plant salal. But florists, for whom this is valuable commercial greenery, know it as lemon leaves, a trade name the leaves may have earned from their pleasant acidic flavor or possibly from a fancied resemblance to the true leaves of the lemon tree. Because these attractive leaves are glossy green, and especially because they are long-lasting, florists everywhere prize them as a decorative accompaniment for floral bouquets. Leafy branches gathered by local brush-pickers are packed and shipped to florists all over the United States.

The following account from a western brush-picker describes the harvesting of salal.

"I'm a brush-picker. I make my living picking sword fern, cedar, salal, and huckleberry foliage, and selling it to packing plants in the area. Salal should be put together spray by spray with odd leaves tucked neatly in between. As long as you don't take more than twenty-five percent of any one plant's foliage, you don't have to worry about hurtin' the shrubbery you pick from. If you make sure your Salal leaves aren't spotted before you pick 'em, you'll find that a bundle weighin' about a pound and a half will bring you about forty-three cents."

❦

This decorative foliage-shrub is also a precious boon to the wild animals of the Northwest region. Domestic animals refuse it as fodder, but for the Roosevelt elk, Olympic wapiti, mountain beaver, deer, and bear, it is an important life-sustaining food.

Salal

SASSAFRAS

Sassafras *Sassafras albidum* (Laurel Family)

During the time of the first settlements in North America, the fragrant sassafras, a native tree with variously shaped leaves, enjoyed its brief burst of fame. After Nicholas Monardes, a Spanish physician, wrote *Joyful Newes Out of the Newe Founde Worlde* in 1574, in which he extolled the medicinal virtues of its roots and wood, the reputation of its healing spread throughout Europe, often initiating sea voyages in search of it. Its wood was valued in England at the exorbitant price of 336 pounds sterling per ton and was one of the first exports sent abroad by Captain John Smith, leader of the Virginia Colony. But later, the renown of its curative power waned and the trade in sassafras ended.

❧

Native Americans were also attracted by the beguiling odor of this tree, specifically, of its leaves, not its wood. They used them medicinally as a purifier of the blood, especially for treating venereal disease, also claiming that they were a "purifier of the spirit," perhaps an early method for dealing with psychosomatic illness.

❧

A Jesuit priest living among the Onondaga of New York—and probably taught by them—wrote the following about sassafras's healing powers: "But

Each part of the sassafras tree has a different smell: the leaves, citrusy; the roots, root beer-like; and its wood, medicinal.

Fill me with sassafras, nurse,
And juniper juice!
And see if I'm still any use!

—Don Marquis
Spring Ode

Sassafras

the most common and wonderful plant...is that which we call the 'Universal Plant,' because its leaves when powdered heal wounds of all kinds in a short time."

❈

For early Americans of the southern mountains, sassafras leaves were a spring tonic, used to cleanse the body of the accumulated ills of winter. One mountain woman advised, "Get some sassafras when the leaves are young and tender; just eat the leaves like you have seen the cows do—the leaves and tender tips—everything."

❈

Today sassafras's medicinal value is described by some as useless, by others, dangerous. Sassafras oil, which is present in all this plant's parts, is known to be extremely poisonous in high dosages. Safrole, the main constituent of this oil, induces tumors in the livers of rats.

❈

In spite of admonishments concerning the toxicity of this tree, the gumbo-loving people of the Mississippi Delta consider filé powder made from the leaves necessary to their lives. Without filé, they say, gumbo is just not gumbo. This Creole dish, a combination of meat, seafood, vegetables, and spices, depends on filé, a culinary legacy from the Choctaws, for flavor and thickening. Though available in all local stores, many families still search out sassafras trees, pick the leaves themselves, then dry and pound them into their own flavorsome powder.

FILÉ POWDER

2-1/2 tbs. dried sassafras leaves
1/2 tsp. whole coriander
1 tbs. dried okra
1/4 tsp. sage

Combine all the ingredients and crush into a fine powder. Store in a tightly lidded jar. Remove gumbo from heat before stirring in this condiment.

SEA GRAPE

Sea Grape   *Coccoloba uvifera*   (Buckwheat Family)

Despite torrid winds, blowing sand, and salt spray, sea grape trees—small, tough, resistant—flourish on sandy beaches from the West Indies to southern Florida. Their large, spherical leaves (which can measure up to eight inches across) not only set them distinctly apart from other trees but give them a strange, unique beauty. These unusual leaves have also earned for this tree the alternative name of platterleaf tree.

🌿

While this tree is evergreen, its leathery leaves do fall, though they do so gradually, not all at the same time in one season as with deciduous trees. And before falling, as they complete their life cycle, they assume rich shades of orange, subdued red, and bronze. Then when the thin, new leaves emerge in their place, they shine with a brilliant, scarlet translucency.

🌿

There is no historic evidence of medicinal or domestic uses for these leaves, nor do they harbor any hidden poisons. Instead, frequently recurring stories mention other, more unusual applications. It is said that early Spanish explorers in Florida utilized these tough leaves in lieu of paper when sending messages. Supposedly the words were meticulously pricked onto the surface of the leaves with the sharp point of a pin. Reportedly, these stiff leaves were sometimes marked and used as playing cards.

🌿

Perhaps inspired by these old-time legends, one inventive Florida teacher painted letters, words, and numbers on these smooth, paperlike leaves, and used them as "flash cards" for her pupils.

※

But the remarkable circular leaves are not this tree's only distinction. Its clustered fruit, purple-red, grapelike berries, is sought for juice, wine, and homemade jelly, a sweet delicacy that rarely, if ever, reaches commercial markets. Because all the fruits in the long clusters do not ripen simultaneously, gathering them presents a problem. Those experienced in harvesting sea grapes spread a sheet beneath the tree, then shake the branches, which causes the ripe berries to fall without disturbing the immature, green ones.

※

This small, fruit-bearing tree is both decorative and enduring, even when planted in wind-tossed seaside gardens. Growing in sturdy groups, sea grapes also serve as a rugged barrier against the erosion of the sandy shore.

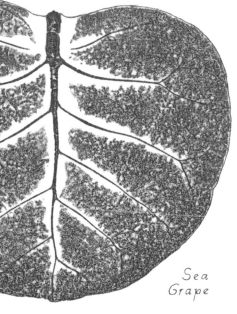

Sea Grape

SEQUOIA

Giant Sequoia   *Sequoiadendron giganteum*   (Taxodium Family)

The giant sequoias of California began their lives many centuries before the birth of Christ; the most ancient trees are now three to four thousand years old. "They are ambassadors from another time," John Steinbeck once observed.

For millions of years, the ancient sequoias flourished throughout the region now known as the United States; they grew from the Pacific coast as far east as New Jersey. The onslaught of the last glacial age all but obliterated these venerable giants. After this massive destruction, the relatively few survivors clung to life in their current habitats, twenty-six isolated California groves where they are now only a vestigial remnant of their former numbers.

Though entire sequoia forests containing untold millions of trees perished beneath the ice, their history has been preserved by their small, awl-shaped leaves. While leaves themselves are among the most ephemeral of nature's wonders, their fossil remains survive seemingly forever, buried deep in the earth's stony crust. By deciphering the petrified messages left by the leaves, geologists can determine the time and extent of the sequoia's former greatness.

Although these trees are dwarfed by the California redwoods, the surviving

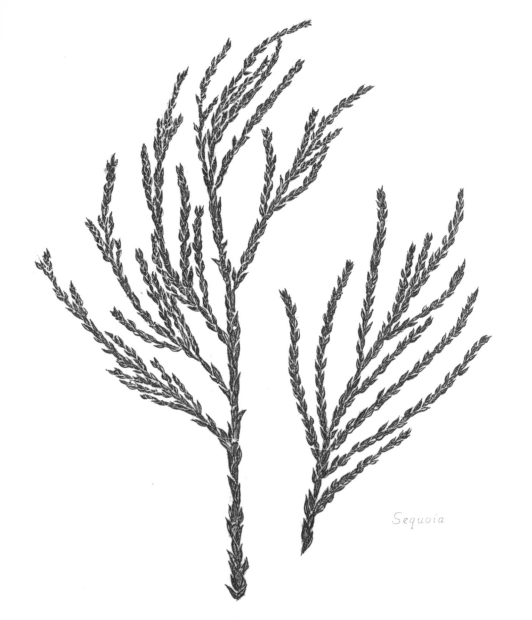

Sequoia

sequoias, in total bulk, are the largest American trees. And the very biggest, with a basal diameter of thirty-six feet, is known as the General Sherman tree. An entire roadway has been cut through the base of this tree.

❧

To preserve this giant tree and all its towering companions, President Theodore Roosevelt created Sequoia National Park in 1890. The National Park Service then provided a troop of cavalry to patrol and guard this heritage. Though shielded in their park against the exploitation of private interests, the sequoias, in their battle against fire, disease, natural disasters, and vandalism, depend on constant vigilance.

❧

The name of this great American tree honors another extraordinary American, George Guess, the son of a white trader and a Cherokee mother. To enlighten his people, Guess devised a method for writing their native language, one character for each of the eighty-six syllables in the Cherokee language. Guess's tribal name was "Sequoyah," which, in Cherokee, was written—"Si quo yah."

❧

To further honor him, Oklahoma chose Sequoyah to represent that state in Statuary Hall in Washington, D.C.

There is always something deeply exciting, not only in the sounds of winds in the woods, which exert more or less influence over every mind, but in their varied waterlike flow as manifested by the movements of the trees, especially those of the conifers. By no other trees are they rendered so extensively and impressively visible, not even by the lordly tropic palms or tree-ferns responsive to the gentlest breeze. The waving of a forest of Sequoias is indescribably impressive and sublime...

—John Muir, A Wind-Storm in the Forests

SILK TREE

Silk Tree   *Albizia julibrissin*   (Pea or Pulse Family)

Treasured for their fernlike foliage and airy, pink flowers, silk trees, lovely Eurasian ornamentals, now grace the southeastern United States and other mild areas in this country. Though all silk trees are essentially trees of warm regions, this particular species is the hardiest of its group, enduring winters as far north as Washington D.C., and, some say, even southern New Jersey. Most others of this group thrive only in the tropical parts of Africa, India, and Central America.

❦

It is a flat-topped, wide-spreading tree with large, many-parted leaves and many-stamened flowers that look like puffs of silken filaments arising from the upper surfaces of the branches. It is the silky, threadlike appearance of these blossoms that has given this tree the descriptive common name of silk tree. But the scientific name of the genus, *Albizia*—its special plant group— honors one member of an aristocratic Florentine family, Filippo degli Albizzi, the Italian naturalist who brought this flowering tree from Constantinople to Italy in 1793.

❦

The silk tree blooms in the daytime,
And sleeps the love-sleep at night.
> —Lady Ki, 8th-century
> Japanese poet
> Manyōshū

Almost as decorative as the flowers, the large leaves, composed of numerous small leaflets (sometimes a thousand or more on each huge compound leaf) are valuable for creating a light, filtered shade. The delicate pattern of shadow cast by the finely divided leaves allows grass and also flowers not dependent on full sun to grow beneath them.

*

As graceful and decorative as these leaves are, in other countries and at other times they have also had practical, everyday uses. In seasons of food scarcity, the aromatic young leaves have furnished humans with subsistance-nourishment, while in some under-developed countries, this foliage is an abundant fodder crop for domestic animals. And plowed into the soil, these living leaves become nutritious organic fertilizer.

*

The featherlike—and useful—leaves of the silk tree, and some others of this same family, exhibit a mysterious behavior called "the sleep of the leaves." The myriad, small leaflets composing the total leaf fold together at night, expanding slowly again with the return of morning light. There have been many theories concerning the cause of this, but so far none have explained it satisfactorily.

> When the Present has latched its postern behind
> my tremulous stay,
> And the May month flaps its glad green leaves
> like wings,
> Delicate-filmed as new-spun silk, will the
> neighbours say,
> 'He was a man who used to notice such things'?
> —Thomas Hardy, Moments of Vision

SilkTree

SOURWOOD TREE

Sourwood Tree   *Oxydendrum aboreum*   (Heath Family)

ourwood, a tree native to the rich woodlands of the southern Appalachians, is a tree for all seasons with glossy leaves and fragrant white blooms. In autumn the lustrous leaves turn a rich, deep crimson. It is a tree suitable for modest home planting, and though originally from the South, it can endure the cold of winter as far north as New Jersey.

❧

Its minuscule white blossoms, standing in rows on slender, drooping stems, earned it the name, lily of the valley tree. And the fragrant honey that bees distill from these small, perfumed flowers is the most prized in the South because of its light color, heavy body, and unique, tangy taste.

Native Americans used a tea of sourwood leaves to alleviate the urinary problems of the tribe's old men. Later, the new settlers found that tea made from "a grasp of sourwood leaves" gathered when red, or as they said, "filled with sun power," together with metal shavings was effective as a diuretic and helpful as a medicine to treat dropsy; for reducing muscular swelling, they made a poultice of leaves and bark. As a general tonic, and also for breaking fevers and chasing chills, the early mountain people drank strong, hot sourwood tea.

❧

Today, its name lives musically in an old Carolina folk song called "On Sourwood Mountain."

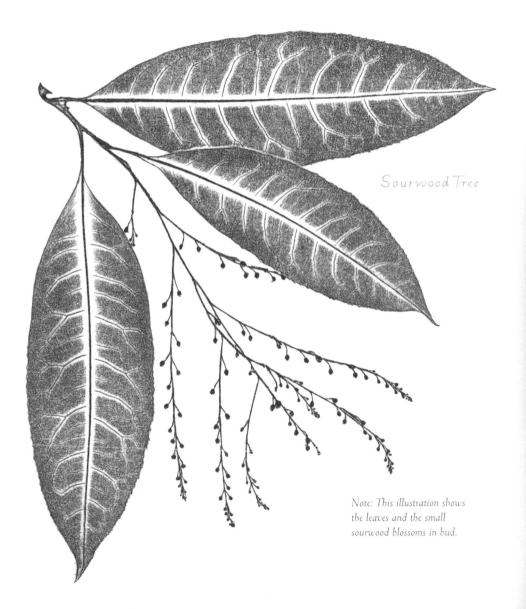

Sourwood Tree

Note: This illustration shows
the leaves and the small
sourwood blossoms in bud.

NORWAY SPRUCE

Norway Spruce   *Picea abies*   (Pine Family)

The Norway spruce, Europe's tallest native, and perhaps the most distinctive of all the needle-clad tribe, is a majestic tree with dark, pendulous branches. From the slender, pointed top, the branches descend in graceful curves to the ground. This stately tree is the only spruce with drooping branchlets and long, hanging cones. Its noble stature, dark color, and unusual cones make it a handsome ornament in parks and yards in the United States and Canada. And as an escape from cultivation, it is also found today in cool northern woodlands.

❧

In its native Norway, where it is also most abundant, an ancient Scandinavian legend relates that the spruce was the original "tree of life" in the Garden of Eden. According to this tale, the tree had juicy fruit, large leaves, and beauteous blossoms until that fatal day when Eve disobeyed and ate its forbidden fruit. To punish the tree for its tempting part in the sin, its fruit was changed to rough, dry cones, and the leaves were shrunken to sharp, pointed needles.

❧

Here in America, the green needles, or leaves, of another spruce, a native one, reputedly had a protective magic—or so

To grow the sweetest and juiciest strawberries, use topsoil taken from a spruce and mulch the plants with spruce needles.

Norway Spruce

this was once believed by the Penobscot of the Northeast. They prudently carried a green spruce twig next to the skin in the belief that it would prevent pain in the side. Perhaps more credibly, the people of Newfoundland cured their toothaches by chewing the resinous buds of these leaves.

🌲

Still more realistically, the lusty loggers and woodsmen of the cold north forgot their troubles by drinking a heady liquor made from spruce needles and twigs boiled together with molasses, then fermented with yeast. Known locally as spruce beer, this brew was harsh, potent, and problem-solving.

🌲

The casual observer who has difficulty distinguishing between spruce trees and firs should remember to look at the shape of their needles. Fir trees have flat needles and spruce trees have square needles. (Note the "f" in fir and flat and the "s" in spruce and square.)

🌲

Another quick, definitive test also exists. Pull a living needle from a twig. If a neat, round dent is left, the tree is a fir, but if a tiny piece of torn bark clings to the needle, and the scar it leaves is ragged, then that tree is a spruce.

One of the most beautiful and exhilarating storms I ever enjoyed in the Sierra occurred in December, 1874, when I happened to be exploring one of the tributary valleys of the Yuba River... I drifted on through the midst of this passionate music and motion, across many a glen, from ridge to ridge; often halting in the lee of a rock for shelter, or to gaze and listen, even when the grand anthem had swelled to its highest pitch, I could distinctly hear the varying tones of individual trees,—Spruce, and Fir, and Pine, and leafless oak...

—John Muir, A Wind-Storm in the Forests

POISON SUMAC

Poison Sumac *Rhus vernix* (Cashew Family)

The poison sumac is truly the worst plant native to North America—one about which nothing good can be said. In the minds of many, all sumacs are poisonous, and it is precisely this small, highly irritating tree that is responsible for this common but ill-founded misconception.

In general appearance, this evil sumac, which usually grows in swamplands, is not so distinctively different from other trees with which it might be confused: it is for this reason that it is not avoided as often as it ought to be. It has, however, certain definite dissimilarities, and the careful observation of them can save much misery.

The long, many-parted leaves, composed of seven to eleven leaflets, are arranged alternately on the branches. The individual leaflets are bright green and smooth-edged—without serrations—and they grow oppositely along a conspicuously red, central stem with one single leaflet at the tip; the mid-vein of each leaflet is also reddish. It is important to notice that the small, greenish-yellow flowers occur in loose clusters on thin, delicate stems. Following the blossoms, the berries are waxy white and grow in small, few-berried clusters, a characteristic that unambiguously differentiates this tree from the harmless sumacs, whose berries are close-clustered, upright, and dark red.

As with other plants in this family, the contact dermatitis that poison sumac confers depends in part on the sensitivity of the person touching it; for some individuals, it is well-nigh deadly. It is estimated that about seventy percent of the population is adversely affected by certain dangerous plants, including this sumac and also poison ivy and poison oak. With prolonged and more frequent exposure to their irritating oil, known as urushiol, an even higher percentage of people are affected. Surprisingly, even dead, dry plants, or those winter-dormant contain this harmful oleoresin, which can be passed onto sensitive persons through smoke, dust, contaminated clothing, even by petting an animal that has brushed against these hazardous plants.

Writing of poison sumac's toxic qualities, Peter Kalm, an eighteenth-century Swedish botanist, compatriot, and protégé of Linnaeus, said, "I have known of old people who were more afraid of this tree than a viper, and I was acquainted with a person who, merely by the noxious exhalations of it, was swelled to such a degree that he was stiff as a log of wood, and could only be turned about in sheets."

Finally, in a masterpiece of understatement, one famous modern book on plants ended its description of poison sumac with this restrained remark: "It is rarely cultivated."

Poison Sumac

Staghorn Sumac

STAGHORN SUMAC

Staghorn Sumac   *Rhus typhina*   (Cashew Family)

As the year winds down and fall arrives, the green, feather-shaped leaves of the staghorn sumac change to shades of orange, scarlet, and deep purple-red. Extolling its brilliant coloring, one author proclaimed, "Almost any writer can describe a beautiful woman, or a baseball game, but William Shakespeare himself could have looked at sumac in early October and been forced to hang up his quill."

When these flaming leaves fall, the bare branches tipped with dense clusters of deep crimson fruits are thought to look like the antlers of a stag, a fancied resemblance that has given this shrub its common name.

Beyond their autumn beauty, these tannin-rich leaves have also had many everyday uses. The Native Americans of Illinois and Miami, recognizing the medicinal value of sumac's tannic astringency, brewed a tea of leaves to control diarrhea; for dropsy, they drank a decoction of leaves, roots, and berries. To check mouth-bleeding, Native Americans around the Great Lakes used an astringent tea of powdered leaves; they also treated venereal disease with this same preparation.

The Native Americans not only cured their ills with sumac leaves, they also smoked them. Several Native American groups made a unique tobacco called *kinikinic*, a mixture of dried sumac leaves and cured tobacco. By combining two-thirds tobacco with one-third sumac leaves, the Native Americans of the Delaware Valley concocted their own distinctive blend. Scouting parties, it was said, could identify these people as Delawares, even at a distance, by the singular scent of their tobacco smoke. Recreational smoking was common among Native Americans, and because sumac leaves smoked as tobacco are hallucinatory, historians believe that they may have been used during rituals designed to communicate with the spirits of their gods.

※

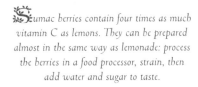

Sumac berries contain four times as much vitamin C as lemons. They can be prepared almost in the same way as lemonade: process the berries in a food processor, strain, then add water and sugar to taste.

Settlers in the Appalachian Mountains also found practical uses for sumac. To cure their headaches and for asthma, they smoked the leaves in a new clay pipe every morning and evening for two weeks; for stomach trouble, they drank beer in which sumac leaves had been boiled. In a very different use, Appalachian tanneries once gathered large quantities of these tannic leaves and twigs for curing the finest grades of pale leather.

※

The small sumac has made one other surprising but delightful contribution. The clustered red fruits detached from their stems can be crushed with sugar and water to make a delicious drink that looks and tastes like pink lemonade.

SWEET FERN

Sweet Fern   *Comptonia peregrina*   (Waxmyrtle Family)

Sweet fern, small, scented and seemingly fernlike, is a low woody plant native to America. It is undeniably sweet, but it is not a fern. It acquired this common name, an understandable misnomer, because each leaf closely resembles one blade of a certain true fern, the small spleenwort. The nature-loving Bishop Compton of Oxford, from whom this plant inherited its scientific name, could not be more distinctly remembered.

❧

This aromatic plant was used by the eastern Native Americans for curing many ills even before the arrival of the colonists. For general weakness, they drank a hot infusion of leaves, a tea they also enjoyed as a pleasant beverage. They rubbed their skin with fresh sweet fern leaves soon after contact with poison ivy or poison sumac, believing that the noxious irritants of these plants would thus be harmlessly dissolved. And to double its effectiveness, they drank a sweet fern decoction at the same time. As an unusual treatment for relieving a toothache, they made a poultice of boiled leaves, then, oddly, merely tied it to the cheek over the offending tooth. For hastening childbirth, the Menominees of Wisconsin administered the juice extracted from fresh sweet fern.

❧

Newly arrived settlers in America learned that infusions and decoctions of these leaves also helped indigestion, colic, after-fever weakness, rheumatism, and dysentery.

Local legend tells that in 1781 an epidemic of the "bloody flux," a severe form of dysentery, devastated the Hudson River town of Rhinebeck, New York, killing many people every day. Still, it was popularly believed that strong infusions of sweet fern saved countless victims. Corroborating this wisdom, the *U.S. Dispensatory* for years listed a decoction of these leaves as a reliable remedy for that illness. The Shakers, the first to gather and market healing herbs in America, recommended preparations of sweet fern leaves for all the same ailments mentioned here.

As with most herbal medicines, these leaves are no longer prescribed, but sweet fern, dried and crushed, is still a sweet-smelling ingredient in potpourris and scented herbal pillows.

Sweet Fern

SWEET GUM

Sweet Gum   *Liquidambar styraciflua*   (Witch-Hazel Family)

The sweet gum, handsome, vigorous, and beautiful in all seasons, is a blessing to the landscape. In summer, it is abundantly clad with starlike green leaves which, in autumn, become a pageant of muted jewel tones—pale yellow, soft red, deep wine, and bronze. In winter, the symmetrically arranged bare branches, thickly hung with long-stemmed seedballs, trace a distinctive silhouette against the sky. Though reliably insect- and pest-free, the only minor fault of this admirable tree is the way it litters the ground with its prickly, brown seedcases.

🌿

The sweet gum gets its common name from the thick, viscous sap which oozes from its bark when the tree is wounded. This sweet substance, gathered by country children as chewing gum, was also recommended as an emollient skin balm in early American folk medicine.

🌿

John Brickell, an Irish doctor who was always interested in botanical healing and traveled in America to observe native plants and local medicines, wrote about the strange and familiar skin problems that were treated with the extract from the sweet gum in the nineteenth century. "The sweet and fragrant gum of this tree," he wrote, "cures the Tetters, Herps, Inflammations, Morphew and other cutaneous disorders." (Today we have other names for some of these illnesses.) Other folk-healers claimed that the leaves of this tree, boiled together with the bark in milk or water, were therapeutic—a country cure for diarrhea and dysentery.

❧

Not only were these beautiful leaves useful for healing; in their fossil form they have documented the long existence of this tree in our part of the world. Stone fossils show that in glacial and even pre-glacial times, sweet gum trees existed in the same regions where they are found today—the southern part of the United States, especially in North Carolina. The same star-shaped leaves, not surprisingly, have bridged the gap between science and poetry. John Gould Fletcher, an American nature poet, lyrically described the sweet gum tree. "The trees splash the sky with their fingers," he wrote, "A restless green rout of stars."

Sweet Gum

Sweetleaf

SWEETLEAF

Sweetleaf   *Symplocos paniculata*   (Sweetleaf Family)

n the early eighteenth century, European botanists, enticed by reports of strange plants, made the long, hazardous voyage to the New World to observe and collect their own specimens. Among those intrepid plantsmen was Mark Catesby, a well-to-do English naturalist who visited North America in 1712. One of the first American plants he described for science was sweetleaf, correctly observing that this shrub or small tree is native to the borders of cypress swamps, edges of streams, and fertile forests of the southern Appalachians. The description of sweetleaf that Catesby included in his book, *History of North Carolina, Florida and the Bahama*

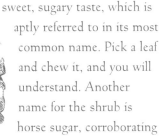

Islands, was so accurate that the great Linnaeus later relied on Catesby's information in his own early writing.

❧

The most unusual characteristic of the leaves of this American shrub is their sweet, sugary taste, which is aptly referred to in its most common name. Pick a leaf and chew it, and you will understand. Another name for the shrub is horse sugar, corroborating the well-known fact that horses have a sweet tooth in general and like to eat this foliage. Cattle, too, devour sweetleaf greedily.

❧

But the most important contribution of these leaves to life in colonial America was their ability to dye wool a fast, bright yellow, a fact confirmed by its alternate names of dyebush and yellow wood. The wool, first steeped in a solution of muriate of tin and cream of tartar, was next boiled in water for three quarters of an hour with a generous quantity of sweetleaf leaves. After a thorough rinsing, the bright wool was hung in the sun to dry.

✳

The golden dye from sweetleaf was sometimes combined with the blue coloring from the indigo plant to produce green. In Cecile Matschat's 1938 book, *Suwanee River, Strange Green Land*, a pioneer woman from Florida describes the dyeing process: "I biled the muslin in a brew made from Indigo plants an' a few pieces of bark from Red Maples. I set the shade with lye from wood-ashes. After the good dried, I dipped it again in yellow dye from the biled leaves and bark of Sweetleaf as grows round the Cypress ponds. Blue and yellow alus makes green," she explained kindly.

✳

The leaves used for this illustration were gathered from a shrub growing in a North Carolina woodland. Mark Catesby, who did so much work in North Carolina, would have approved.

SYCAMORE

Sycamore   *Platanus occidentalis*   (Plane-Tree Family)

Though not the tallest, the sycamore is the most massive of all trees of the eastern and central U.S. By the time the tree celebrates its first century, it has often become hollow, developing cavities where birds build nests and small animals find shelter. To achieve its great girth and spread, it then continues to grow slowly for 500 to 600 more years.

❧

While it is not uncommon for cavernous sycamores to serve as dens for raccoons and owls, one exceptional tree in West Virginia was for three years the cavelike home of two pioneering brothers, Sam and John Pringle. Though this sheltering tree no longer exists,

another tree marks that historic spot.

❧

The exfoliating bark of the sycamore, which exhibits irregular patches of gray, tan, and white, is unlike the wrapping of any other tree. Three thousand years ago, the Greek poet Homer observed the piebald bark of a related sycamore and in his immortal *Iliad* wrote, "Performing sacrifices to the gods under a dappled sycamore."

❧

When young, the maplelike leaves are clad with fine, sharp hairs that fall off as the leaves mature. When this happens, the air is filled with pointed but almost imperceptible particles, an occurrence that people throughout history

For the ancient Egyptians, the sycamore tree was worshiped as the sacred home for the goddess Nuît. The dead, crossing the desert on their way to the afterlife, would approach the tree and call, "O, sycamore of the Goddess Nuît, let there be given to me the water which is in thee." The goddess would then bestow bread, fruit, or water to the traveler who, upon accepting it, could never turn back.

have noted with alarm. Galen, the second-century Greek physician, observed it and warned, "The dust or downe that lieth on the leaves is to be taken heed of, for if it be drawn in with the breath, it is offensive to the windpipe by its extreme drinesse, and making the same rough and hurting the voice...also the sight and hearing if it falls into the eyes and ears."

✻

Centuries later the American pioneers avoided settling near sycamore trees, believing that the constant irritation of the lungs resulted in "consumption," the illness we know today as tuberculosis.

Though we now know the "shedding" of the sycamore is not the cause of tuberculosis, there is no denying that the lungs and nasal passages of sensitive persons can be adversely affected by it.

✻

In contrast, sycamore leaves have also been credited with healing and protective powers. Pliny, the Roman naturalist, claimed that the leaves and bark "make an ointment for gatherings and suppurations" (abscesses), while an old superstition offered other beneficial though certainly questionable information. It advised that leafy branches of the plane tree (an alternate name), hung in the house, drove away "bats, snakes, scorpions, and all other noxious vermin."

In Clanenagh in County Laois, Ireland, there is a sycamore called the money tree whose bark is embedded with thousands of coins hammered into it by the superstitious and believed to contain a continual source of holy water.

Go, little book, and wish to all
Flowers in the garden, meat in the hall
A bin of wine, a spice of wit,
A house with lawns enclosing it,
A living river by the door,
A nightingale in every sycamore!

—Robert Louis Stevenson
Envoy

Sycamore Tree

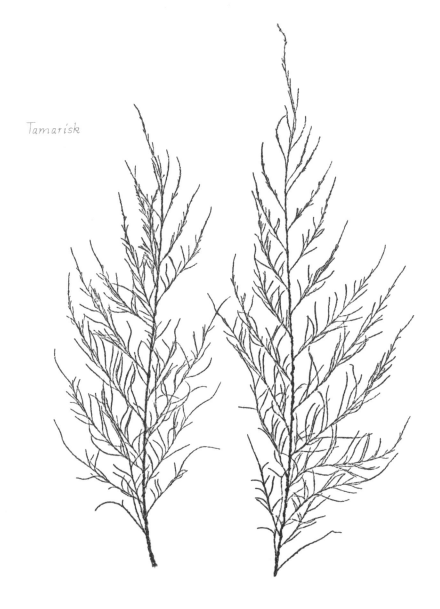

Tamarisk

TAMARISK

Tamarisk   *Tamarix gallica*   (Tamarisk Family)

The ancients knew the tamarisk. The pages of old records, the writings of a Greek physician, and the works of Roman and British herbalists all proclaim its name and fame.

🌿

The words of the Bible are green with this tree, and they tell that Abraham planted one in Beer-sheba, that Saul sat beneath another in Gibeah, and that the bones of Saul and his sons were buried beneath a tamarisk in Jabesh.

🌿

Dioscorides, the Greek physician, also knew this tree, and believed that "the decoction of the leaves being drank with wine doth melt the spleen, and being gargalized in the mouth doth help the paines of the teeth." He also recommended infusions of the leaves for "such as breed lice and nitts."

🌿

Pliny, the Roman naturalist, prescribed an ointment made from the leaves for treating "nightfoes and chilblanes." He further optimistically promised that if tamarisk was boiled in wine, beaten up with honey, and applied to cancerous sores, they would "quickly be healed." Other ancient wisdom maintained that a sprig of tamarisk broken off without touching iron or the ground would relieve a bellyache if pressed against the body "between the tunic and the girdle."

🌿

And believing it medicinal, John Gerard, the sixteenth-century English herbalist, proclaimed that tamarisk had a "cleansing and cutting faculty," adding also, "It is good for a hard spleen"—the same cure for this disorder that Dioscorides had discussed fifteen centuries earlier. After the pronouncement by Gerard, because of his exalted reputation, thousands of tamarisks were cultivated in England.

In spite of the tamarisk's reputed healing power, some also called it an unlucky, accursed tree because it never bore fruit. It was seen as a plant of evil repute, and the feathery branches were used to garland criminals when they were put on shaming public display. It was also thought that tamarisk leaves mixed with the urine of an ox and a eunuch had the power to cause impotence.

During the 1820s, this Eurasian tree was introduced into the United States, where it is sometimes called salt cedar because of its superficial resemblance to red cedar and its preference for growing near saltwater. Today on the Gulf of Texas, tamarisk is being planted on man-made, offshore dredge islands where its deep-ranging, sinewy roots prevent the erosion of the fragile, sandy shoreline. And as a pink-flowered ornamental of almost vaporous beauty, it increasingly graces gardens in eastern and midwestern America.

High noon behind the tamarisks—
the sun is hot above us—
As at Home the Christmas Day is breaking wan.
They will drink our healths at dinner—
those who tell us how they love us,
And forget us till another year be gone!

—Rudyard Kipling, Christmas in India

TEA

Tea   *Thea sinensis*   (Tea Family)

ook upon this leaf with awe. It is a wellspring of legends, an ancient healer, and a banisher of nodding sleep. Even more, it is a leaf of destiny; ponder its power. It has precipitated rebellion and war, shaken an empire, and sparked the start of a new nation. It has built fast fleets and established world trade routes. Today the beverage habits of half the world are borne on this leaf. It is tea, the same gentle leaf once known to the Chinese as "the gift of Heaven."

The plant bearing these remarkable leaves is an evergreen shrub, a relative of the flowering camellia, and is believed native to the part of the world encompassing Assam, Burma, Thailand, Vietnam, and China. Over the many centuries that this plant and its uses have been known, legends surrounding its origins have gathered. One myth tells of Bodhidarma, a sixth-century Buddhist sage who fell asleep during a night-long prayer vigil. Enraged at his own weakness and frailty of faith, he tore off his offending eyelids, casting them on the ground. Where they fell, a tea bush sprang up— a bush whose powerful leaves could

For an effective skin wash for minor sores, cuts, and abrasions, place an entire tea plant in very hot water and steep for about an hour. Apply to affected area as needed.

Tea

Thank God for tea! What would the world
do without tea?—how did it exist? I
am glad I was not born before tea.

—Sydney Smith
Lady Holland's Memoir

One cup of tea contains more fluoride than a glass of fluoridated water.

hold sleep at bay.

❋

Tea—the infusion of these leaves—goes back at least five thousand years, and for the first five hundred years of its existence it was considered a medicine. The ancient Chinese believed it beneficial for "abscesses that come about the head, for ailments of the bladder; it dissipates heat caused by the inflammations of the chest, quenches thirst, lessens the desire for sleep, gladdens and comforts the heart." Some of these antique claims are still true.

❋

It was the Chinese who introduced this many-powered beverage to the Western world—to Holland in 1610; France in 1636; Russia in 1638; and finally England in 1658. By the end of the seventeenth century, tea-drinking was commonplace.

❋

Today tea is the world's most popular beverage and, per cup, the least expensive. Each country has its own favorite type and manner of drinking. Ninety-eight percent of the tea consumed in the West is black (made from fermented, heated, and dried leaves). Most Asians, however, prefer their tea leaves green (unfermented), and their beverage hot, plain, and unsweetened, except for Tibetans, who consider it delicious with ghee—a semi-fluid clarified butter—and salt. For North Africans, fresh mint and sugar are essential. Westerners take it with a variety of sweeteners, such as sugar and honey; in Russia, jam is commonly used. Americans alone with their passion for cold summer drinks, like tea sweet, tinkling with ice and laced with lemon.

❋

THYME

Thyme *Thymus vulgaris* (Mint Family)

To the ancient people of the lands surrounding the Mediterranean—Egyptians, Greeks, and Romans—thyme, a small shrub, delicate but tough and wiry, was a fragrant delight. That its exceptional scent was considered alluring is clearly evident from a line in a fifth-century B.C. Greek drama in which an actor, alluding to thyme, gently asks:

Who could forbear to kiss
A girl who's wearing this?

※

However enticing the scent of the

In the Middle Ages, noblewomen sewed sprigs of thyme—a symbol of courage—onto the scarves of their Crusade knights.

minuscule leaves, the importance of their antiseptic uses once was more compelling. Early classical writings tell that the air of Greek temples was purified by burning thyme as incense. Greek and Roman texts praised its ability to drive out infection—or as the Roman, Pliny, put it, "thyme, when burnt, puts to flight all venomous creatures." He continued by listing twenty-eight disorders for which he recommended thyme as a remedy.

※

Authentic or not, there were many early medical uses for these small but powerful leaves—for inducing urination and menstrual discharge, loosening the congestion of chest and lungs, and, by

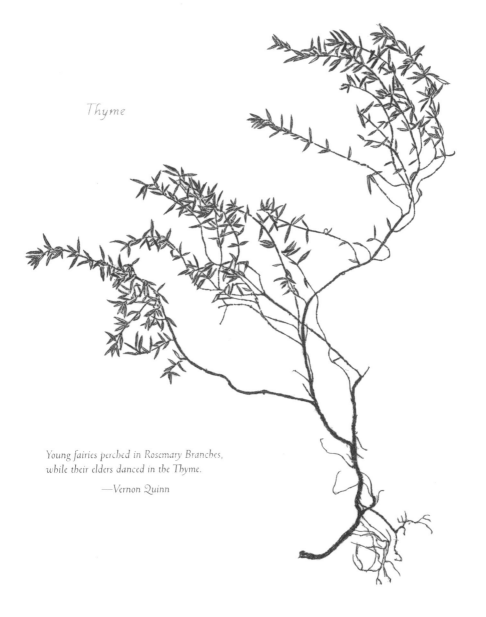

Thyme

Young fairies perched in Rosemary Branches,
while their elders danced in the Thyme.

—Vernon Quinn

being merely sniffed, they were said to benefit epilepsy and prevent "frensye and nightmare."

※

Folk medicine from the Middle Ages to the present has continued to believe in the curative value of thyme in teas and syrups for coughs, colds, and sore throats, also claiming decoctions of thyme with honey effective for combating that dread childhood affliction, whooping cough.

※

Skeptics and disbelievers in the credibility of folk medicine may be interested to learn that scientific analysis has revealed that thymol, the chief ingredient in the essential oil made from thyme, has twelve times the antiseptic power of carbolic acid, a potent disinfectant. Even

To dry thyme: Collect plants just before flowering, tie them together in bunches, and hang to dry in a warm and airy place.

Here of Sunday morning
My love and I would lie
And I would turn and answer
Among the springing thyme.

—A. E. Housman
The Shropshire Lad

today, medicine containing thymol is prescribed for the treatment of hookworm. Cough medicines and gargles, too, include thymol among their active ingredients; in soap, dentifrices, and medicines, it masks strange or unpleasant odors.

※

Ask French cooks about thyme and they'll describe *gigot d'agneau*, French roast leg of lamb, or stews like *pot-au-feu* and *cassoulet*, all fragrantly flavored with thyme. Ask Americans and they may give you a treasured recipe for Manhattan clam chowder or poultry stuffing, neither of which could even exist without thyme.

TREE OF HEAVEN

Tree of Heaven   *Ailanthus altissima*   (Quassia Family)

The unconquerable tree of heaven—or ailanthus—springing forth in such unlikely places as between bricks or in deserted alleyways vigorously embraces even the most unfavorable city environments. Though a native of China, it is now completely at home in most parts of the United States, where it is the fastest growing tree, advancing up to eight feet in one year. Reflecting the ailanthus's serene disregard for soil or location, its large leaves, sometimes three feet long, spread with a tropical luxuriance, lend an exotic richness even to the harshest urban surroundings.

❧

It was believed in the early 1800s that these long, hardy leaves absorbed "malarial poisons" and were for a long time in demand for urban plantings. Then, after several unexplained epidemics in American cities, people began to wonder if these poison-absorbing leaves might also be returning these same toxic substances back into the atmosphere and, to protect themselves, started to destroy them. These unfounded fears gradually subsided, and the popularity of the ailanthus returned.

❧

Contrary to the one-time belief that these leaves were harmful, it was reported in 1887 in *American Medicinal Plants* by Milspaugh that respected authorities endorsed an extract from ailanthus leaves. Although the nausea accompanying this medicine when taken orally was most disagreeable, the drug was effective

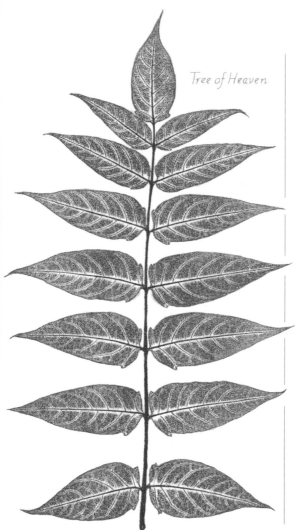

Tree of Heaven

given in a tincture for palpitations of the heart, asthma, and epilepsy, and as an emetic or cathartic for treating dysentery and diarrhea. An alcoholic extract of leaves and bark drove out tapeworms and an injection of it helped gonorrhea.

The way this tree with exotic foliage came originally to America is an interesting story. The leaves are unappetizing to most insects except for the larvae of the silk-producing Cynthia moth. When the culture of the common mulberry-leaf-eating silkworm *(Bombyx mori)* was threatened by disease, the tree of heaven was brought from China to Europe to feed to Cynthia worms. In Europe and America this plan failed in establishing a new silk industry. However, today the tree of heaven lends grace and greenery to our cityscapes.

TULIP TREE

Tulip Tree   *Liriodendron tulipifera*   (Magnolia Family)

"Lily Tree Bearing Tulips" is the English meaning of the impressive scientific name *Liriodendron tulipifera* which was once bestowed on this tree by Linnaeus, the great botanist. Also referred to as the tulip magnolia, tulip poplar, yellow poplar, or canary whitewood tree, the tree can be found from Massachusetts to Michigan and south to Louisiana and northern Florida. The "tulips" that it bears, large cup-shaped green flowers splashed with orange, grow from the ends of its branches. This magnificent flowering tree is one of the tallest of all native broadleaf trees in the eastern United States, reaching a height of 80 to 100 feet and a trunk diameter of up to 50 feet. One growing in Bradford, Virginia, the largest on record, reaches an awesome 146 feet.

According to fossil records preserved in stone, the tulip tree grew throughout the world and was native in many parts of Europe but became extinct there during the last great ice age. It finally appeared again in Europe around the late 1680s, this time as an introduced species. Still growing there today, the tulip tree enriches many parks and gardens. One of the most appreciated imports from America, it is prized for its noble stature, exotic green flowers, and thick covering of odd-shaped leaves. They are between 4 to 6 inches across, very smooth on both sides, lustrous and dark green above and paler below. Variously described as "end-notched," "saddle shaped" and "bitten off," the leaves are so unique that they can never be mistaken for any other species.

❋

Medicinal benefits reputedly lay within these singular leaves. Native Americans and the early settlers pounded the leaves of the tulip tree into a poultice to ease their aching heads, while an ointment of the leaf-buds crushed in bear grease was said to soothe a variety of skin disorders.

❋

Throughout the eighteenth century, the strange and interesting plants native to the New World attracted inquisitive botanists and herbalists from Europe. Among them was John Brickell, an Irish doctor who, like the others, was moti-

vated by a lively curiosity about America. Recording his findings on the

tulip tree in *Natural History of North Carolina*, he wrote: "The planters frequently made an oyntment of the buds which is excellent good to cure all manner of inflammations, scalds and burns." He also added, "The cattle are very fond of its leaves which gives a very good taste to the milk."

❋

More recently this tree inspired Sacheverell Sitwell, an English poet, to honor it with a poem.

❋

Whose candles light the Tulip Tree?
What is the subtle alchemy
That builds an altar in one night
And touches the green boughs
   with light?
Look at the shapèd leaves below
And see the scissors mark they show,
As if a tailor had cut fine
The markings of their every line.

Tulip Tree

VIRGINIA CREEPER

Virginia Creeper   *Parthenocissus quinquefolia*   (Vine or Grape Family)

The sign on a stake protruding from the pot that held a tendrilled plant stated clearly, "American Vine." Under other circumstances it would not be unusual —except this was in a street market at the foot of the Rialto Bridge in Venice, Italy. Why it was identified in English is a mystery. In that country, as elsewhere in Europe, this "American Vine" is treasured as a garden plant, an interesting, imported horticultural specimen.

❧

Here in the United States, we call it Virginia creeper and it is doubtful that we would've sold it as a potted plant. The plant is a familiar sight, native and ubiquitous. As its common name implies, it creeps, and also trails and climbs, aided by its disk-tipped tendrils. It is a slender, lovely vine whose five-parted leaves gracefully cover many random spots with living green. And in late autumn, when its leaves turn vivid scarlet and it is still bearing its deep blue berries and brilliant leaves, the Virginia creeper is a welcome sight in the bare, gray woods.

❧

The leaves of the Virginia creeper played an important role in American folk medicine. Though very unpleasant in taste, they once had some use as emetics, purgatives, and sweat-producing diaphoretics. They were also considered mildly stimulating. Inhaling the juice of the leaves held to the nostrils reportedly cured headaches, while an infusion of leaves and berries, taken warm, lessened the pain of even the most severe headaches. For another herbal cure, fresh leaves boiled in vinegar and applied warm as a poultice gave relief to those suffering with a bad spleen, or with a "stitch in the side." For an annoying health problem, a strong decoction of the leaves rubbed directly on the scalp destroyed head lice in children.

✽

And finally one last use only rarely mentioned in herbal medicine. An old belief claimed that a strong tea of Virginia creeper leaves healed even the worst hangover.

Virginia Creeper

Black Walnut

BLACK WALNUT

Black walnut *Juglans nigra* (Walnut Family)

Incredible as it may seem, the American black walnut—a tree with many excellent uses—is at war with the rest of the plant world. Science now confirms what country people have known all along, that this tree, in its desperate struggle to preserve its own existence, kills all life-threatening competitors. By means of a substance called juglone, which is present in the roots and leaves, it effectively eliminates other nearby trees, especially fruit trees. Even this tree's seedlings are not immune from its ruthless attack—unexpectedly sinister behavior in the peaceable kingdom of plants.

❈

However, in spite of these antagonistic ways, the black walnut tree has much to recommend it, including its dark wood for fine furniture and carvings, and its distinctively flavored nuts always in demand by bakers and confectioners.

❈

In early America the leaves were valued for eliminating unwanted insects, such as ants, houseflies, and even bedbugs. To rid the house of fleas, southern mountain folk advised, "Circle the infested area with black walnut leaves; in a short time the fleas will be gone."

Because of the "brain-like" appearance of its meat and the "skull-like shape" of its shell, the walnut was prescribed by the Doctrine of Signatures for the treatment of head wounds and mental illnesses.

The leaves were also used to dye cloth and hair permanent shades of brown. By varying the mordants—substances used to fix color—used with the leaves, the cloth could be dyed in a range of colors, from golden brown to cinnamon to a deep dark brown. With strong solutions made from walnut leaves, aging country women once gave their gray hair a fresh, youthful boost. (Interestingly, it is the juglone in the leaves, so deadly to other trees, that gives these leaves their dyeing power.)

Even more importantly, black walnut leaves, rich in astringent tannin, had many medicinal uses. A decoction of leaves, because of its power to bind together irritated tissues, was often applied to diseased skin and open sores. As a gargle, it also helped to heal mouth irritations, including canker sores and sore throats. During the Civil War, a strong, costive tea from these leaves was administered to soldiers as a swift, effective remedy for diarrhea and dysentery.

An amusing bit of seventeenth-century herbal fantasy claimed, "If the leaves be taken with salt and honey, they help the biting of the mad dog, or the venom or infectious poison of any beast."

Waxmyrtle

WAXMYRTLE

Waxmyrtle   *Myrica cerifera*   (Waxmyrtle Family)

The American colonists used the waxy berries of this native shrub, also known as candleberry, to illuminate the night. Growing prolifically along the coastal plain from New Jersey through Florida and on to Texas, this evergreen provided an abundance of gray berries for the resourceful colonists who estimated that one pound of them immersed in hot water would yield four ounces of fragrant wax, enough for one gray-green, hand-dipped candle. A slightly different form of this shrub, commonly called bayberry, grows northward to Newfoundland.

❦

The colonists along the East Coast used the leaves, which have a spicy aroma, in sachets to scent clothes stored in chests and to banish fleas from the beds of their dogs. And long before window screens were common, they hung branches of these strong-smelling leaves in their bedrooms to repel insects. They also relied on these leaves to flavor soups and stews, especially those made with seafood.

❦

This useful American shrub interested John Brickell, a visiting doctor from Dublin, who recorded his medicinal

To obtain the fragrant wax from waxmyrtle berries, boil them in water until the wax rises to the surface. Carefully skim off and, when slightly cool, soften into a candle mold.

findings. In 1737, he wrote, "The Bay Tree [his name for waxmyrtle] not only yields a Wax for Candle making, but is useful in Chirurgery, the Leaves are of a bitter, astringent Nature, but grateful to the Stomach, and resists Vomiting; when made into a Pulse, help all Inflammations, the stinging of Bees and other venomous Beasts." And although not mentioned by Brickell, others claimed that waxmyrtle leaves in tea were effective for cleansing the liver.

＊

Native Americans also used these leaves medicinally. The Choctaws of Louisiana boiled the leaves and young stems to reduce fevers, while the Gulf Coast Houmas made a tea of waxmyrtle leaves to expel worms; others employed them as a mild emetic. In a more unusual use, the southern Creeks and Seminoles concocted them into a charm-medicine for preventing illness and for exorcising the spirits of their dead.

＊

The Shakers gathered and sold these leaves, recommending them in teas to treat scurvy, as a poultice for cuts and scratches, and powdered as snuff to clear nasal congestion and catarrh.

＊

Today, the importance of waxmyrtle leaves is diminished. However, crafts-people interested in natural materials do still use them to dye their wool a soft, gray-green color.

WEEPING WILLOW

Weeping Willow   *Salix babylonica*   (Willow Family)

This pendulous Chinese tree, now planted and esteemed all over the world, is especially loved in America. With neither impressive economic importance, nor a wealth of blossoms, nor a harvest of luscious fruit to recommend it, the weeping willow is prized simply for the elegant beauty of its hanging, leaf-strung branchlets. Like all willows, this one likes its feet wet and grows most luxuriantly where its romantic image is doubled in the reflection of a nearby pool.

This tree is sometimes called Napoleon's willow because two of them were mirrored in the stream near the French emperor's grave on the island of St. Helena. Cuttings from these historically famous trees, now grown to full size, are treasured specimens in botanical gardens around the world, including those in the Royal Gardens of Melbourne, Australia.

The weeping willow, because of its unique grace, is frequently celebrated in art and poetry, especially in the nature writings of the Chinese, in which plants are endowed with a spiritual relationship to man. In this translation of an old poem, the author Ouan Tsi shows his sensitive observation of a willow leaf as it reflects, in this case, the ever-recurring sorrow of a young man disappointed in love.

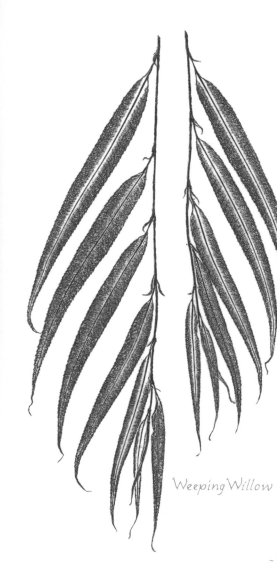

Weeping Willow

The Leaf on the Water

~

The wind tears a leaf from the willow tree;
it falls lightly upon the water,
and the waves carry it away.
Time has gradually effaced a memory from
       my heart,
and I watch the willow leaf drifting
      away on the waves.
Since I have forgotten her whom I loved,
I dream the day through in sadness,
lying at the water's edge.

But the willow leaf floated back
      under the tree,
and it seemed to me
that the memory could never be effaced
      from my heart.

Ouan Tsi (1007–1072)

WHITE WILLOW

White Willow   *Salix alba*   (Willow Family)

Willows put down their roots, spread forth their branches, and make themselves at home worldwide, from polar cold to tropical heat, from highlands to lowlands, and from east to west. No other family of trees encompasses such a wide and varied territory.

❀

Originally from Eurasia, white willows earned their name from the light look of the leaves when the sun strikes their silken surfaces. Shakespeare observed the pale-leaved willow, and in *Hamlet* picturesquely declared, "There is a Willow grows aslant a brook/That shows its hoar leaves in the glassy stream."

❀

Not only beautiful ornaments, wil-lows hold with their tenacious roots the fragile banks of streams. In England, they give their timber for cricket bats, and in all countries, the light wood was used for artificial limbs before the advent of plastic.

❀

Medicinally, the willow tree is one of the great benefactors of the world, its history a healing thread linking ancient and modern times. The Greeks knew the willow, and their renowned physician, Dioscorides, claimed its leaves stayed bleeding as in nosebleeds, alleviated deafness, and were an effective

Willows whiten, aspens quiver,
Little breezes dusk and shiver.

—*Alfred, Lord Tennyson*
The Lady of Shalott

White Willow

The poor soul sat sighing by a sycamore tree,
Sing all a green willow.
Her hand on her bosom, her head on her knee,
Sing willow, willow, willow.

—William Shakespeare, Othello

contraceptive. He went on to claim, "A decoction of them is an excellent fomentation for ye gout." For fifteen centuries, European herbalists repeated his advice.

*

Native Americans discovered the pain-dulling magic of willow leaves mashed into a poultice for toothaches and brewed into a tea for headaches. Later, American folk healers recommended the astringent leaves to cure dysentery, control bleeding, and to treat eczema and gangrene, even cancerous sores. Willow substances, simply because of their bitter taste, were once even considered a substitute for fever-reducing quinine. Appalachian Mountain people trusted willow leaves and bark to break fevers and relieve the pain of rheumatism, neuralgia, and gout, uses which in the light of modern medicine were perhaps this tree's most significant contribution.

*

Willow's effectiveness is due to an element called salicin, which in the form of salicylic acid was introduced in the 1800s for reducing pain, fever, inflammation and swelling. In 1899, a still more effective analgesic derived from salicylic acid was accidentally discovered: its name was aspirin, the most successful manufactured drug in all of pharmaceutical history. Although synthetically produced today, aspirin owes its origin to the beneficent willow tree.

There once was a Willow, and he was very old,
And all his leaves fell off from him, and left
him in the cold;
But ere the rude winter could buffet him
with snow,
There grew upon his hoary head a crop of mistletoe.

All wrinkled and furrowed was this old
Willow's skin,
His taper finger trembled, and his arms
were very thin;
Two round eyes and hollow, that stared but
did not see;
And sprawling feet that never walked, had this
most ancient tree.

—Juliana Horatia Ewing, "The Willow Man"

WINTERGREEN

Wintergreen   *Gaultheria procumbens*   (Heath Family)

For an old-fashioned Pennsylvania Dutch quilting bee, serve sparkling pink wintergreen wine. For a less stimulating beverage with a clean, wintergreen fragrance, prepare a tea by pouring boiling water over fresh or dried leaves and letting it steep for two days. The taste of wintergreen drawn from the essence within the leaves can also enhance candy and chewing gum and mask the unpleasantness of some medicines.

The flavorsome leaves of wintergreen, a small, woodland shrub, also enjoyed a reputation as a valid source of medicine. Even before the European settlers arrived, the Native Americans were using the leaves to treat their ills. The Potawatomis of Michigan concocted a tea to break fevers and alleviate the pain of rheumatism, while the Menominees of Wisconsin and the Ojibwas of Lake Superior drank it for lumbago. The Delawares and the Shinnecocks of Long Island used it for kidney ailments.

In colonial America, in the markets of Philadelphia, wintergreen leaves from the Pine Barrens of New Jersey were sold for one cent a bunch. These leaves in tea mitigated the pain of toothaches, headaches, gout, and sciatica and also the discomfort of colds and grippe; as a gargle, they soothed sore throats. Leaves crushed as a poultice matured boils, healed "felons" (an infection usually found on a finger), and were an all-purpose treatment for any external inflammation.

The knowledgeable Shakers picked, dried, and marketed wintergreen leaves, which they claimed could be used as a stimulant, astringent, diuretic, and emetic, and though this is unmentioned by others, they also believed them valuable for colic in infants.

The active principle, oil of wintergreen, distilled from the fresh leaves by steam, contains methyl salicylate, almost the same curative agent as that in aspirin, and is reliably known to be beneficial for muscular aches and pains. The leaves and twigs of black birch (Betula lenta) yield an oil with the same aroma, properties, and uses. This oil, always called wintergreen oil, whether truly from wintergreen of alternatively from black birch leaves and twigs, was at one time included in the U.S. Pharmacopoeia. This oil is now synthetically produced.

Wintergreen

WITCH HAZEL

Witch Hazel   *Hamamelis virginiana*   (Witch-Hazel Family)

This shrub is wild, weird, and witchy. Botanists, sober souls that they are, assure us that the name has nothing to do with witches, claiming it comes from an old Anglo-Saxon word, "Wican," meaning "weak" or "flexible." But learned opinions aside, this odd shrub is indeed witchlike, with ways that can hardly be called normal. In late fall, even into winter, when all its woodland companions are hibernating, this eccentric shrub opens its spidery yellow flowers. Still more strange, it explosively shoots out its polished black seeds fifteen, twenty, even thirty feet into the quiet woods of late autumn. Two other common names, winterbloom and snapping hazel, emphasize its singularity.

Henry Thoreau, himself an odd but eminently sane American naturalist writing in the nineteenth century, was impressed by this unusual shrub and commented, "There is something witchlike in the appearance of witch hazel which blooms in October and November with its irregular and angular spray, and petals like furies' hair or small ribbon streamers. Its blossoming, too, at this irregular period when other shrubs have lost their leaves as

> Witch-hazel blossoms
> in the fall,
> To cure the chills and
> Fayvers all.
>
> —Ernest Thompson Seton,
> The Sanger Witch

well as blossoms, looks like witches' craft."

⚜

The Native Americans used the leaves of this peculiar shrub as medicine, preparing from them a liniment for rubbing on bruises, inflammations, and aching backs. They may have passed on their healing lore to the colonists, who lessened the excessive mucous discharge of feverish colds in steamy sweat baths of leafy witch hazel branches. They stopped internal hemorrhages and diarrhea by drinking a brew of the leaves; for internally bleeding hemorrhoids, the powdered leaves were used as an astringent snuff. In all these uses, witch hazel's binding power was the active principle, yet modern chemistry has disputed these claims, saying that its essence is quite inert. Whether beneficial or useless, the fact remains that the demand for witch hazel as a

bracing aftershave capable of healing minor cuts has never ceased. The southern Appalachians are the chief source of dried leaves for producing this herbal extract.

⚜

Though the former uses of these leaves were mainly medicinal, the Iroquois of New York State did use them to make a pleasant tea to drink with meals. The French Canadians, too, concocted a drink with these leaves, but judging by the satanic name they gave it, it seems unlikely that they liked it very much. They called it *café du diable*—devil's coffee.

Bottled witch-hazel water is not as effective as witch-hazel water made from fresh leaves. To make your own, bring 2-1/2 cups of water to a boil, add 1 tablespoon of powdered leaves and boil for 10 to 12 minutes. Strain liquid and allow to cool. Apply directly onto skin.

Witch Hazel

ACKNOWLEDGMENTS

For the many and varied gifts I have been given during the preparation of this book, I am deeply grateful to all the generous and knowledgeable people without whose concerned help these leaves would never have flourished. Their gifts include plant specimens, local identifications, botanical data, helpful books, introductions that opened doors, old folklore, technical information, and above all—encouragement. I give thanks for each valuable contribution.

Extra thanks go to certain people, and they know the reasons—Silvana Settanni, Lilian Morrison, Hilda Martin, Any Staeger, my sister Joan Hopkins, nimble-fingered Maureen Lake, and especially my long-suffering husband, Albert Vitale.

FAMOUS NAMES IN THE HISTORY OF PLANTS

❧

Brickell, Dr. John, 1710-1745?
Irish doctor and herbalist, traveled in America, wrote *Natural History of North Carolina*, 1737.

Culpeper, Nicholas, 1616-1654.
English apothecary, astrologist and herbalist, wrote *The Complete Herbal* and *English Physician*.

Darwin, Charles, 1809-1882.
English naturalist, author of *Origin of Species*.

Dioscorides, Pedanius, A.D. 40-90.
Greek pharmacologist and physician to the Roman Army, wrote *De Materia Medica*.

Druids
An order of priests and teachers of religion in ancient Gaul and Britain who regarded the oak and mistletoe with veneration.

Galen, A.D. 131-200.
Greek imperial physician in Rome; his writings on medicine and drug plants were accepted as authority by Greek, Roman and Arabic doctors.

Gerard, John, 1545-1612.
English botanist, barber-surgeon and author of the still-famous *Herbal* or *General Historie of Plants*.

Grieve, Mary A.
A Fellow of the Royal Horticultural Society (London) with an encyclopedic knowledge of medicinal plants.

Hippocrates, c.460-c.377 B.C.
Greek physician, called "The Father of Medicine," wrote eighty-seven medical treatises, including many on treatment by diet and drugs.

FAMOUS NAMES

Kalm, Peter, 1716-1779.
Swedish botanist, protégé of Linnaeus, traveled in North America, wrote *Survey of Natural History.*

Linnaeus, Carolus (Carl von Linne), 1707-1778.
Physician and author, known as "Father of Systematic Botany," wrote *Species Plantarum*

Mattioli, Pierandrea, 1501-1577.
Italian physician, wrote Commentaries on the *Six Books of Dioscorides.*

Michaux, François André, 1770-1855.
French botanist, traveled in America observing plants, especially trees, wrote *North American Sylva,* 3 volumes, 1810.

Parkinson, John, 1567-1629.
London apothecary and king's herbalist, author of *Theatrum Botanicum, An Herbal of Large Extent,* which contained descriptions of 3,800 plants.

Pliny (Gaius Plinius, Secundus), A.D.23-79.
Roman scholar, known as "Pliny the Elder," wrote *Historia Naturalis.*

Shakers
An American branch of English Quakers; established socialist communities in the U.S. and were the first to gather, package, and market garden seeds and medicinals.

Theophrastus, Eresios, 372-287 B.C.
Greek philospher, author of earliest still-surviving treatise on plants, *Enquiry Into Plants.*

BIBLIOGRAPHY

Aikman, L.
Nature's Healing Arts.
National Geographic Society, 1977.

Anderson, F. J.
An Illustrated History of Herbals.
New York: n.p., 1977.

Ashley, R.
Cocaine: Its History, Uses and Effects. New
York: St. Martins Press, 1975.

Austin, R. and U. Koichiro.
Bamboo.
New York and Tokyo: n.p., 1970.

Bailey Hortorium, Cornell University,
Hortus Third.
New York: Macmillan, 1976.

Bailey, L. H.
Standard Cyclopedia of Horticulture.
New York: Macmillan, n.d.

Brickell, J.
Natural History of North Carolina.
Rpt. Murfreesboro: n.p., 1968.

Brown, J. H.
Early American Beverages.
New York: Bonanza Books, 1966.

Caron, M., and H. J. Clos.
Piante Medicinali.
Milan: Mondadori, 1966.

Coates, A. M.
Garden Shrubs and Their Histories.
New York: Dutton, 1964.

Conci, C.
Natura Viva.
Milan: n.p., 1966.

Culpeper, N.
Nicholas Culpeper's Complete Herbal.
London: Foulsham, 1955.

Favretti, R., and P. DeWolf.
Colonial Gardens.
Barre: n.p., 1972.

Fernald and Kinsey.
*Edible Wild Plants of Eastern North
America.* New York: Harper, 1943.

BIBLIOGRAPHY

Foley, D. J.
The Flowering World of Chinese Wilson.
New York: n.p., 1969.

Frazer, J. G.
The Golden Bough.
New York: Macmillan, 1935.

Gerard, J.
Gerard's Herbal. 1636,
Rpt. London: Howe, 1927.

The Herbal, or General History of Plants.
Rpt. New York: Dover Publications,
1975.

Gibbons, E.
Stalking the Healthful Herbs.
New York: McKay, 1966.

Grandjot, W.
*Reisefuhrer Durch Das Pflanzenreich
der Mittelmeerlander.*
Bonn: Schroeder, 1962.

Grieve, M., and C. F. Leyel., ed.
A Modern Herbal, 2 vols.
New York: Hafner, 1974.

Griggs, B.
Green Pharmacy.
New York: n.p., 1982.

Gunther, R. T., ed.
The Greek Herbal of Dioscorides.
New York: Hafner, 1959.

Hermann, A.
*Die Alten Seidenstrasse Zwischen
China and Syrien.*
Berlin: Weidemann, 1910.

Hui Lin Li.
*Origin and Cultivation of Shade
and Ornamental Trees.*
Philadelphia: n.p., 1963.

Hutchins, R.,
Insects.
Englewood Cliffs: Prentice Hall, 1966.

Jarvis, D.
*Folk Medicine. A Vermont Doctor's
Guide to Good Health.*
New York: Holt, 1962.

BIBLIOGRAPHY

Johnson, H.
International Book of Trees.
New York: Simon & Schuster, 1973.

Joigneaux, P.
*Le Livre de la Ferme et des
Maisons de Campagne.*
Paris: n.p., 1865.

Kennedy, D.
The Cuisines of Mexico.
New York: Harper & Row, 1972.

Keyes, J.
Chinese Herbs.
Rutland: n.p., 1976.

Kingsbury, J.
Poisonous Plants of the U.S. and Canada.
New York: Prentice Hall, 1973.

Kreig, M.
Green Medicine.
Chicago: Rand McNally, 1964.

Krochmal, A., and C. Krochmal.
A Guide to the Medicinal Plants of the U.S.
New York: Quadrangle, 1950.

Krutch, J.
Herbal.
New York: Putnam, 1965.

Leach, M.
*Standard Dictionary of Folklore, Myth,
Mythology and Legend.*
New York: Funk & Wagnells, 1973.

Lehner, E., and J. Lehner.
Odysseys of Food and Medicinal Plants.
New York: Farrar, Straus & Giroux,
1973.

Lesch, A.
Vegetable Dyeing.
New York: Watson Guppill, 1970.

Lewis, W., and E. Lewis.
Medical Botany.
New York: Wiley, 1977.

Lowenmo, R.
Arbres et Arbustes de Parcs et de Jardins.
Paris: Fernand Nathan, n.d.

Matschat, C.
Suwanee River, Strange Green Land.
New York: n.p., n.d.

BIBLIOGRAPHY

Menninger, E.
Seaside Plants of the World.
New York: Hearthside Press, 1964.

Messegue, M.
Of Men and Plants.
New York: n.p., 1973.

Metro, A. and C. Sauvage.
La Nature au Maroc.
Rabat: La Société de Sciences, 1955.

Moldenke, H. N., and A. Moldenke,
Plants of the Bible.
Waltham: n.p., 1952.

Peattie, D. C.
Flowering Earth.
New York: Putnam, 1942.

Trees of Eastern and Central U.S.
Boston: Houghton Mifflin, 1948.

Pliny.
The Natural History.
New York: n.p., 1962.

Polo, M.
Travels of Marco Polo.
Willow: n.p., 1958.

Potter.
Potter's New Cyclopedia of Botanical Drugs and Preparations.
Rustington: n.p.,1968.

Radford, E., and M. Radford.
Encyclopedia of Superstitions.
Hole, ed. London, 1948.

Robertson, S.
Dyes from Plants.
New York: Nostrand & Rheinhold, 1973.

Sargent, C.
Manual of the Trees of North America.
Boston: Houghton Mifflin, 1959.

Scully, B. A.
A Treasury of American Indian Herbs. New York: Crown, 1970.

Shurtleff, W. and A. Aoyagi
The Book of Kudzu.
Brookline: Autumn Press, 1977.

Smith, F.
Chinese Materia Medica.
Revised. Shanghai: n.p., 1911.

BIBLIOGRAPHY

Tanaka, S.
The Tea Ceremony.
Tokyo and San Francisco: Kodansha
International, 1973.

Taylor, N.
Plant Drugs That Changed the World.
New York: n.p., 1965.

Thompson, W.
Herbs That Heal.
New York: Charles Scribners Sons, 1973.

Ukers, W.
All About Tea.
New York: n.p., 1935.

Vogel, V.
American Indian Medicine.
Norman: University of Oklahoma
Press, 1970.

Walker, W.
All The Plants of the Bible.   ·
New York: Harper, 1957.

Weiser, F.
Handbook of Christian Feasts and Customs.
New York: Harcourt, Brace and World,
1947.

West E., and L. Arnold.
Native Trees of Florida.
Gainesville: University of Florida
Press, 1946.

Wiggenton, E., ed.
Second Foxfire Book.
Garden City: Anchor Books, 1971.

Wyman, D.
Shrubs and Vines for American Gardens.
New York: Macmillan, 1949.

Yasuda, K.
A Pepper Pod.
New York: Knopf, 1947.

INDEX

✻

INDEX

INDEX

INDEX

INDEX

INDEX

INDEX

INDEX

This book has given a passing glance into the surrounding green and living world where, in myriad ways, every leaf has touched life.

-And Then-

Every blade in the field,
every leaf in the forest
lays down its life in its season
as beautifully as it was
taken up

—Henry David Thoreau,
1817-1862